FTCE
Music K-12
SECRETS

Study Guide
Your Key to Exam Success

FTCE Test Review for the
Florida Teacher Certification Examinations

Dear Future Exam Success Story:

Congratulations on your purchase of our study guide. Our goal in writing our study guide was to cover the content on the test, as well as provide insight into typical test taking mistakes and how to overcome them.

Standardized tests are a key component of being successful, which only increases the importance of doing well in the high-pressure high-stakes environment of test day. How well you do on this test will have a significant impact on your future, and we have the research and practical advice to help you execute on test day.

The product you're reading now is designed to exploit weaknesses in the test itself, and help you avoid the most common errors test takers frequently make.

How to use this study guide

We don't want to waste your time. Our study guide is fast-paced and fluff-free. We suggest going through it a number of times, as repetition is an important part of learning new information and concepts.

First, read through the study guide completely to get a feel for the content and organization. Read the general success strategies first, and then proceed to the content sections. Each tip has been carefully selected for its effectiveness.

Second, read through the study guide again, and take notes in the margins and highlight those sections where you may have a particular weakness.

Finally, bring the manual with you on test day and study it before the exam begins.

Your success is our success

We would be delighted to hear about your success. Send us an email and tell us your story. Thanks for your business and we wish you continued success.

Sincerely,

Mometrix Test Preparation Team

Need more help? Check out our flashcards at: http://MometrixFlashcards.com/FTCE

TABLE OF CONTENTS

Top 20 Test Taking Tips

1. Carefully follow all the test registration procedures
2. Know the test directions, duration, topics, question types, how many questions
3. Setup a flexible study schedule at least 3-4 weeks before test day
4. Study during the time of day you are most alert, relaxed, and stress free
5. Maximize your learning style; visual learner use visual study aids, auditory learner use auditory study aids
6. Focus on your weakest knowledge base
7. Find a study partner to review with and help clarify questions
8. Practice, practice, practice
9. Get a good night's sleep; don't try to cram the night before the test
10. Eat a well balanced meal
11. Know the exact physical location of the testing site; drive the route to the site prior to test day
12. Bring a set of ear plugs; the testing center could be noisy
13. Wear comfortable, loose fitting, layered clothing to the testing center; prepare for it to be either cold or hot during the test
14. Bring at least 2 current forms of ID to the testing center
15. Arrive to the test early; be prepared to wait and be patient
16. Eliminate the obviously wrong answer choices, then guess the first remaining choice
17. Pace yourself; don't rush, but keep working and move on if you get stuck
18. Maintain a positive attitude even if the test is going poorly
19. Keep your first answer unless you are positive it is wrong
20. Check your work, don't make a careless mistake

Music Theory, History, and Literature

Music in the Medieval era

Music of the Middle Ages was dominated by vocal music that could be separated into two separate genres. Sacred music included Gregorian chant and masses, and secular music included music for dance and entertainment, such as that of the troubadours and trouvères. Gregorian chant had melodies that were free flowing with no distinct meter, melismatic, and largely monophonic, sung by unaccompanied voice or choir. The sacred music of the Middle Ages evolved with the development of organum, an early form of polyphony in which voices were sung in parallel motion. Masses were also an important religious ritual and featured non-imitative polyphony. The most important form of Medieval polyphony was the motet, which spanned both sacred and secular genres. By the end of the Middle Ages, secular music became the driving force of musical development, and the music of troubadours and trouvères saw drone accompaniment and had regular meter, syncopations, polyphony, and harmony.

Musical importance of the mass

As one of the most important services of the Roman Catholic Church, the mass was a driving force of musical development in the Medieval and Renaissance eras. The liturgy of the Ordinary was most often set to music, and musical advancements were applied to the composition of the mass. By the Renaissance era, polyphony was common, musical notation had been refined, and complete masses were written by a single composer; the first mass by a known composer was Machaut's Mess de Notre Dame. As a large-scale form, the mass continued to appear in many composers' oeuvre, including that of Dufay, Josquin, Palestrina, Haydn, Mozart, Beethoven, Schubert, Weber, Berlioz, Verdi, Wagner, Fauré, and others. Although the genre declined through the twentieth century, composers continue to set the mass to new musical settings (Hindemith, Stravinsky, Bernstein, etc.) The Ordinary includes six sections and is outlined as follows: Kyrie, Gloria, Credo, Sanctus, Benedictus, and Agnus Dei.

Medieval motet vs. Renaissance motet

The motet was a major musical form of the Medieval and Renaissance periods that emerged from medieval organum and clausulae. The Medieval motet featured a tenor line derived from plainchant with one or more upper voices in French or Latin. The tenor vocal line usually had a short, repeated rhythmic pattern, while the upper voices had contrasting, lively upper voices. The texts of the upper voices were sometimes independent and in a different language from the tenor line. The Renaissance motet, in contrast, referred more to a genre of music than to a certain form or structure. By the mid-fifteenth century, the motet was known as a polyphonic setting of any sacred Latin text, not restricted to the liturgy. Composers of the Renaissance introduced imitation, homophony, and four-part harmony to the motet.

Polyphony, homophony, and monophony

The terms polyphony, homophony, and monophony all refer to a certain texture of music. Polyphony refers to a texture of music in which all voices or parts hold similar musical prominence or interest. This can be thought of as several distinct melodic lines occurring at the same time. The rhythm of each line in polyphonic music moves independently of each other. Homophony also has several voices or parts, but melodic interest is reduced to a single voice or part. All other voices or parts support the main melody as

- 2 -

accompaniment and move together in rhythmic likeness. In this way, homophony can be thought of as any form of melody and accompaniment texture. Monophony also centers on a single melodic line; however, unlike homophony, it does not have supplemental accompaniment parts. A prime example of monophony is plainchant in which a single line of melody embodies the entire work itself.

Characteristics of Baroque music that Classical composers rejected and reacted against

In the Baroque era, music was stylistically ornate and heavily ornamented. During this period, tonality was established, counterpoint was invented, and the size, range, and complexity of orchestrations were expanded. By the end of the Baroque era, music innovations became so complex that a new aesthetic was formed in reaction against the overly embellished Baroque aesthetic. Homophony replaced polyphony, simplicity replaced complexity, and gentler sentiment replaced strong passion. With the prominence of homophony, Classical music featured a slower harmonic rhythm than the ornate Baroque music that featured a linear bass line. Classical composers emphasized a natural melody above textural complexity and wrote music with a clear phrase and period structure. Instead of keeping a musical piece in one affect as in the Baroque period, Classical composers introduced stylistic contrasts within a piece.

Nationalistic composers

The Nationalist movement was a facet of the Romantic era during the late nineteenth and early twentieth centuries in which music evoked the national or regional character of a place. Composers used folk music in their compositions either as a direct quote or as a framework for the composition of melodies and rhythms that resemble folk music of the area. Nationalistic composers who represented Russia include Glinka, Borodin, Balakirev, Mussorgsky, and Rimsky-Korsakov. Nationalistic composers who represented Czechoslovakia include Smetana, Dvořák, and Janáček. Composers who famously represented Norway and Finland, respectively, are Grieg and Sibelius. Composers who represented England include Elgar, Vaughan Williams, and Holst. Composers who represented Spain include Albéniz, Granados, and de Falla. Composers who represented Hungary include Bartók and Kodály. Nationalistic composers who represented the United States include Ives, Harris, Gershwin, and Copland.

Nineteenth-century debate over program music and absolute music

In the nineteenth century, music philosophers debated the value of program music versus absolute music. Programmatic music, or music that represented non-musical images or ideas, flourished in the Romantic era with program symphonies, symphonic poems, and character pieces with descriptive titles. Examples of Romantic-period program music include Don Quixote by Richard Strauss, Danse Macabre by Camille Saint-Saëns, Symphonie Fantastique by Hector Berlioz, and The Sorcerer's Apprentice by Paul Dukas. Absolute music was defined by opponents of program music as instrumental music that existed apart from extra-musical references, able to move audiences solely on the purity of the music itself. Proponents of programmatic music argued that music alone could not express anything and that music needed associations for audiences to fully grasp musical expression. Recent scholars acknowledge that the divide over program music and absolute music is not as distinct as once believed, and is open to interpretation.

Impact of valved horns and trumpets

Before the nineteenth century, horns had a range limited to the notes of the overtone series and to crooks or hand-stopping techniques that changed the pitch of the instrument. Although the hand-stopping technique added a wider range to the horn, tone and volume were highly variable. The trumpets of the Classical era were more limited than the horns; although they also had a range limited to the notes of the overtone, hand-stopping techniques could not be used to add a wider range because of the length of the early trumpet. The invention of the valved horn and keys for the modern trumpet allowed players to play chromatically throughout their entire range. Composers began to incorporate more brass into their orchestral writing and, as a result, brass instruments became essential instruments in any orchestra with leading parts and solos. The orchestral sound of the nineteenth century increased substantially in power and capacity, and composers such as Wagner, Strauss, Stravinsky, and Mahler became known for their tremendously large orchestrations and vast scope of sound.

Impressionist movement

The Impressionist movement in music was influenced by the synonymous movement in visual arts by painters such as Monet, Cézanne, Degas, Manet, and Renoir, in which subtle brushstrokes obscured any sharp lines to give a general "impression" of a scene without precise details. French composer Claude Debussy developed a musical equivalent in which sound defied strict harmonic rules and soft instrumental colors focused on constant movement without distinct sectional borders, giving the audience a similar effect as in Impressionist art of a general experience rather than one that draws attention to specific details. Melodies tended to center around a single pitch without much climax, similar to the individual brushstrokes utilized by Impressionist painters of the time. Debussy was a key Impressionist composer; other composers who have worked in the Impressionist aesthetic include Maurice Ravel, Béla Bartók, Oliver Messiaen, György Ligeti, and George Crumb.

Arnold Schoenberg

Arnold Schoenberg (1874-1951) was an Austrian theorist and painter, and one of the most influential composers of his time. Schoenberg developed the 12-tone technique of music in which all 12 pitches of the chromatic are treated as equal, rejecting the conventions of traditional tonality. The 12 pitches are ordered into a series that becomes the basic structure for the composition. The pitches can be in any range or duration, but they must be introduced in the composition in that order. Schoenberg's revolutionary system of composition broke away from the traditional tonality of the twentieth century and abandoned any hint of a tonal center. The impact of Schoenberg's 12-tone system of composition continued in the music of Milton Babbit, Pierre Boulez, Charles Wuorinen, Anton Webern, Karlheinz Stockhausen, Alban Berg, Luigi Nono, Roger Sessions, and multiple other composers.

Neoclassical movement

At the end of the nineteenth century, Romantic music reached the height of expressive emotionalism with the large-scale works of program music by composers such as Tchaikovsky, Liszt, and Mahler. The beginning of the twentieth century brought about Modernism and the rejection of tonality by experimental composers such as Schoenberg, Boulez, Berg, and Webern. Neoclassicism was a trend of the twentieth century that emerged as a reaction to the emotionalism of the late Romantic era and the abandonment of tonality in the early-twentieth century. Composers of the neoclassical movement sought a return to the order, restraint, clarity, and formal balance of the music of the eighteenth century. Neoclassical music usually featured restraint, lighter texture, objectivity, a transparent melodic line, and a call to music of the past. Prominent composers of the neoclassical movement include Paul Hindemith, Igor Stravinsky, Richard Strauss, Sergei Prokofiev, Manuel de Falla, and Aaron Copland.

Minimalist movement

Minimalism began as a compositional movement in the late 1960s, as a reaction to the traditional goal-oriented, narrative, and representational music of the previous centuries. As an extension of experimental music, minimalist music often features compositional techniques that emphasize the process of music

- 4 -

rather than motion towards a goal. Minimalist composers sought to create music that uses a minimal amount of notes, minimal instruments, and minimal focal points, so that the music could become more a wall of sound than a goal-oriented mission. Minimalist music tends to have a consonant harmony, perpetually repeated patterns or drones, interlocking rhythmic phrases and rhythms, and gradual transformation. In minimalist music, the form tends to be continuous without well-defined separate sections; notes may be added to a repeating pattern slowly so that the resulting effect of the music becomes somewhat hypnotic. Representative minimalist composers include Steve Reich, Terry Riley, Philip Glass, John Adams, and La Monte Young.

Latin jazz

Latin jazz is a style of jazz that originated in the late 1940s when musicians merged the rhythms and instruments of Afro-Latin music with American jazz music. The two prominent sub-genres of Latin jazz are Afro-Cuban jazz and Afro-Brazilian jazz. Afro-Cuban jazz incorporated Cuban rhythms such as the mambo and the habanera with elements of bebop. Afro-Cuban bass lines featured distinctive syncopated rhythms labeled as either a 2-3 clave or 3-2 clave. Afro-Brazilian jazz incorporated rhythms of the samba with music of Europe and America. A new style of samba known as bossa nova featured a laid-back singing style, increased textural complexity, and a distinctive rhythmic pattern known as the bossa nova clave. Famous Latin jazz musicians include Mario Bauzá, Luciano Pozo, Frank Grillo, W. C. Handy, Dizzy Gillespie, Antonio Carlos Jobim, and João Gilberto, among others.

Bossa nova movement

The bossa nova movement originated in Rio de Janeiro, Brazil, in the late 1950s and combined elements of the popular Brazilian samba with elements of American jazz. It soon became popular in the United States and then became an international sensation. Bossa nova is characterized by a laid-back singing style, complex harmonies, and a distinctive rhythmic pattern known as the bossa nova clave. The music of bossa nova often features acoustic guitar as a principal instrument and also includes bass, drums, voice, and piano. The bossa nova rhythm, often notated in duple meter, starts with a downbeat but is otherwise syncopated to give a swaying feeling rather than a strong, measured pulse. Central figures of the bossa nova movement include Antônio Carlos Jobim, João Gilberto, Vinícius de Moraes, Sérgio Mendes, Roberto Menescal, and Nara Leão. Famous tunes include "Chega de Saudade," "Girl from Ipanema," "Desafinado," "Corcovado," "Águas de Março," and "Mas Que Nada."

Blues

Music of the blues originated through African-American work songs that were brought over to the United States in the nineteenth and early-twentieth centuries. The rise of the blues occurred approximately around the time of the emancipation of slaves in the U.S., especially in the Mississippi delta and east Texas. Elements such as the call and response format, the unaccompanied voice, and accompaniment styles all have roots in traditional African music. By the mid-twentieth century, the blues had a standard 12-bar harmonic progression: I-I-I-I-IV-IV-I-I-V-IV-I-I. The blues also utilizes the blues scale that features a lowered third and a dominant seventh, called the "blues notes." Music usually centers on a melancholy emotion, with instrumental and vocal techniques such as moans, growls, and cries to express that emotion. Famous blues musicians include Blind Lemon Jefferson, Charley Patton, Blind Blake, Blind Willie McTell, Leadbelly, Bukka White, Big Bill Broonzy, Muddy Waters, B. B. King, and T-Bone Walker.

Leitmotif

The term leitmotif is used to identify a reoccurring motivic fragment that musically represents some part of a musical drama, usually a person, place, or idea. The leitmotif must be clearly recognizable by its melody, harmonic progression, or rhythm. In the context of an opera, the leitmotif becomes a useful tool for composers as character development and the unfolding of the story. In a musical drama, the leitmotif can reinforce the action taking place onstage, as well as recall an event or person from a previous scene. The leitmotif can also be modified through thematic transformation and even combined with other leitmotifs to suggest a change in the narrative and the characters' relationships. The term is most often associated with Wagner's later operatic works, although he preferred the terms Grundthema and Hauptmotiv instead.

Harmonic language

Harmonic language before Wagner was dominated by the rules of diatonicism and straightforward voice leading. By the middle of the nineteenth century, composers started to explore ideas of chromaticism and common tone relationships rather than strong root progressions. The arrival of Wagner's Tristan und Isolde brought a major change to the harmonic language of the past and signaled a new era of modern compositional techniques. In the four-hour opera, chromaticism plays a prominent role in the dissolution of typical harmonic expectation. Now known as the Tristan chord, the leitmotif of the main character reveals a functionally ambiguous tritone chord (f-b-d#'-g#'), which instead of resolving progresses to another equally chromatic and dissonant tritone chord. Wagner's use of harmonic suspension, full chromaticism, polyphony, and range of colors in Tristan und Isolde paved the way to the modern collapse of traditional tonal writing and to the advent of experimental, atonal compositions of the twentieth century such as those of Bruckner, Mahler, and Schoenberg.

Organum

Organum is considered to be one of the earliest forms of polyphony and appeared in the Medieval period. Organum was based on a cantus firmus and began as improvised voices that duplicated the original melody. Organum types included parallel voices at the octave and parallel voices at the fifth below. Composers adjusted the lines to avoid tritones as necessary. Organum expanded to include contrary and oblique motion, as well as free or florid organum in which the tenor chant held notes and upper voices decorated the tenor with phrases of varying length. In the twelfth century, the development of the discant in organum moved the compositional techniques further towards polyphony as voices became increasingly complex and independent. By the thirteenth century, the motet had replaced organum as a major polyphonic genre.

Greek tragedy

Ancient Greek tragedies hold an important influence on the modern opera and theatre of today. Many of the initial developments of modern opera and theatre were based on the classic form. The elements of a classic tragedy include plot, character, thought, diction, melody, and spectacle. In a classic Greek tragedy, the hero often has a goal but encounters limits through human frailty, the gods, or nature, and usually encounters suffering. The characters of a tragedy must show essential qualities or morals that remain consistent throughout the plot. Thought is often displayed through a Greek tragedy to drive the plot line and to reveal key plot elements. Diction must be clear and serve the lines of the tragedy as one the most important elements of tragedy. Melody is subservient to words and should only be used to accessorize the plot. Spectacle refers to the setting of the drama and, like melody, should be used as an accessory.

Opera seria vs. opera buffa

By the end of the seventeenth century, opera as a musical form had been widely accepted. Two genres appeared as the philosophical focus as the new century turned its attention to the Enlightenment. Thinkers and composers of the Enlightenment held that opera should reflect ancient Greek values such as clarity and unity, structure, and propriety; the opera seria that arose during this time focused on tragic and serious subjects that were historical rather than mythical. The structure, number of singers, and plot line were structured so that the action usually took place in three acts with alternating arias and recitatives, and the number of characters usually numbered six or seven, with two to four main characters. Opera buffa, in contrast, focused on humorous and light-hearted elements. There was often a wide range of characters, and spoken dialogue replaced recitative. The form was less structured and often featured prominent orchestral and instrumental parts. Music tended to be faster and helped portray comic elements of the plot line, such as laughter and sneezing.

Authentic musical modes

The authentic musical modes are commonly used in modern times and have origins in the Medieval musical tradition as well as the Greek musical tradition. The most commonly known authentic musical modes are Ionian, Dorian, Phrygian, Lydian, Mixolydian, Aeolian, and Locrian. The Ionian mode is also known as the major scale in modern musical theory. Dorian is similar to the natural minor scale, but has a raised sixth scale degree. Phrygian is similar to the natural minor scale, but has a lowered second scale degree. Lydian is similar to the major scale, but has a raised fourth scale degree. Mixolydian is similar to the major scale, but has a lowered seventh scale degree. Aeolian is also known as the natural minor scale in modern musical theory. Locrian is similar to the natural minor scale, but has a lowered second scale degree and a lowered fifth scale degree.

Classical sonata form

The sonata form has been a key compositional structure since the Classical era. Usually referring to a convention within a single movement of a sonata or symphony, the sonata form features three main sections: the exposition, development, and recapitulation. The melodic and harmonic themes of the movement are usually introduced in the exposition. The initial first subject is introduced in the tonic key, while the second subject is usually in the dominant or relative minor key. In a typical sonata form, a bridge or a short transition connects the first and second subjects. In the development section, the thematic material from the exposition is altered, modified, and transformed through mood, key, and modulations. The development section of a sonata form introduces tension that demands resolution; tension builds until the beginning of the recapitulation, in which tonal balance is reinstated with a shortened version of the initial subject and the second subject, this time in the tonic key instead of the dominant or relative minor. A coda may round out the sonata at the end.

Classical symphonic form

The symphony was a major compositional form in the Classical era and refers to a large musical work usually for orchestra or another combination of instruments in four movements. The classical symphonic form has a fast first movement, a slow second movement, a dance form in the third movement, and a fast fourth movement. The first movement is usually in sonata allegro form, which contains an exposition, development, and recapitulation. The second slow movement is usually in a gentle, lyrical ABA pattern or a theme and variations. The third movement is typically in a dance form such as the Minuet and Trio or the Scherzo. The fourth movement is typically in Rondo form, or Sonata Rondo form, in which a principal theme in the tonic key alternates with new episodes: ABACADA...etc.

Opera vs. oratorio

Opera began as an art form in the late-sixteenth century and consisted of a staged dramatic work with singers and orchestra. Oratorios began as an art form in the seventeenth century and became popular in part because of the success of opera and because of religious bans on secular operas during Lent. Both opera and oratorio are large-scale musical works that feature dramatic, musical, and narrative elements. The two forms both utilize solo vocalists, chorus, ensembles, and orchestras. However, opera is usually theatrically staged, while oratorio is not. Also, oratorio usually centers on a religious or ethical subject, while opera usually centers on historical, mythological, or other secular plot lines. Famous operas include Jacopo Peri's Daphne, Gioacchino Rossini's Barber of Seville, Giacomo Puccini's Madame Butterfly, W.A. Mozart's The Marriage of Figaro, Guiseppe Verdi's La Traviata, and Georges Bizet's Carmen. Famous oratorios include G.F. Handel's Messiah, Joseph Haydn's Creation, and Felix Mendelssohn's Elijah.

Waltz form

The waltz is a dance form that has been popular since the eighteenth century and features triple meter in a lively tempo. The term literally means "to turn about," and musical aspects of the waltz help dancers feel the refined and fluid motion of the turn. In waltz time, emphasis is on the downbeat, while the other two beats create a sense of floating, as on the dance floor. Early forms of the waltz featured two simple repeated phrases of about eight measures. As the dance evolved, the waltz became longer in form and more complex, with introductory material as well as a coda. The ballroom dance achieved popularity across all of Europe and reached its height of fashion with the Viennese waltz. Representative composers of the Viennese waltz include Joseph Lanner, Johann Strauss, Franz Schubert, Frédéric Chopin, Franz Liszt, Johannes Brahms, and Pyotr Tchaikovsky.

Changes giving rise to the Renaissance movement

The period from 1400 to 1600 was a time of major change not only in Western musical history, but also in Western history in general. The 1400s marked the end of the Hundred Years' War, the fall of the Byzantine Empire, and the end of the Great Schism. During the Renaissance, religious conflicts emerged through the Reformation, European colonialism expanded, and a middle class grew in many European nations. As a result of the Ottoman Turks' victory, displaced Byzantine scholars brought ancient Greek writings with them to other European countries, and the Western world had access to the plays and histories of ancient Greece for the first time. Renaissance art featured classical Greek and Roman ideals of humanism, clarity, and clean form. As a result, music of the Renaissance featured Greek modes, clarity of vocal lines, harmonic consonance, imitative counterpoint, and expressivity. The printing press was also invented during this time, so music became widely available to the expanding middle class.

Baroque music

Music of the Baroque era, from 1600 to 1750, was influenced by the rise of rationalism in the philosophy of the time. Composers sought to portray emotions through objectivity rather than subjectivity, and the expression of any one piece or movement was limited to a single affect. Thorough bass was prominent during the Baroque era, and a Baroque ensemble would typically read music and improvise on a figured bass, also known as continuo. Ornamentation was used heavily in the Baroque period and consisted of embellished notes of a musical line. These included trills, mordents, and grace notes that were rarely written out but instead were improvised by the performers. Famous composers of the Baroque era include Claudio Monteverdi, Girolamo Frescobaldi, Arcangelo Corelli, Antonio Vivaldi, Domenico Scarlatti,

François Couperin, Jean-Phillippe Rameau, Georg Philipp Telemann, G.F. Handel, J.S. Bach, and Henry Purcell.

Influence of African song and dance on Latin American music

The historically large African population found in the Caribbean region near South America has had a substantial influence on the development of Latin American music. Common features of African music include call and response singing, repeated and improvised musical figures, polyrhythm, and the use of African instruments such as congas, rattles, thumb pianos, claves, and drum ensembles. Calypso music, originally developed in Trinidad, is a popular song and dance form in the Caribbean. Typically played with a steel drum band, calypso music is witty, lively, and humorous. The rumba is another African song and dance form now popular in Cuba that uses conga drums and sticks. The rumba has a three-part form with fast polyrhythms, and includes improvised verses and repetitive call and response sections. The merengue, prominent in both the Dominican Republic and Haiti, is a popular song and dance style in a swift duple meter. Instruments with some African influences include the double-headed tambora drum and the metal guayo scraper.

Pre-Colombian indigenous musical culture of South America

Most of the Pre-Colombian indigenous musical culture of South America known today revolves around the Inca of Peru and the Aztecs of central Mexico. The Spanish conquerors of the sixteenth century recorded the role of music in these highly developed civilizations that produced public ceremonies, professional musicians, and musician-specific educational institutions. Aztec and Inca rulers employed musicians who were responsible for new compositions and performances of large repertoires. Standards of performance were held high, and a mistake in a ceremonial performance or dance could mean death. Since no evidence has been found of a Pre-Colombian musical notation, little is known about the actual sound and style of their music. However, evidence of Aztec and Inca instruments reveals those such as the huehuetl and teponaztli types of drums, gourd rattles, flutes and panpipes, clay jingles, wood and conch shell trumpets, bone rasps, and ocarinas.

Mambo

The mambo is a song and dance genre of music that stems from the Afro-Cuban movement of the 1940s. The form developed in Cuba with influences from Mexico and the USA, as well as those from European dances and African rhythms. The genre soon became popular in Latin America and crossed over to the United States, where the mambo dance became a ballroom staple, especially in New York City. Mambo is performed by an ensemble that usually consists of double bass, bongo, tumbadora, trumpets, guitar, and voices. The mambo rhythms are moderate to fast, and features distinctive riffs for the rhythm section and brass instruments. Cowbells often play strong syncopations over the second beat in a mambo ostinato, while the conga drum varies struck tones through unaccented strokes, strongly accented strokes, and open tones.

Early Broadway songwriters and American musical theater

The first Broadway songwriters of the 1920s included Irving Berlin, Jerome Kern, the Gershwins, Harold Arlen, Oscar Hammerstein, Richard Rodgers, and Cole Porter. American musical theater of the early twentieth century was intricately tied to the New York music industry called Tin Pan Alley, a geographical location where musicians and composers came together to create popular new songs for the working class as a reaction against upper-class parlor music. The style borrowed heavily from the jazz scene as well as African-American sounds and themes. The success of Tin Pan Alley songs depended on large-scale production and stage shows on Broadway, and the first Broadway shows were loosely related singing, dancing, and vaudeville music from Tin Pan Alley. Historians mark Show Boat (1927) by Kern and Hammerstein as the first full-fledged Broadway musical with a complete beginning-to-end plot.

Appalachian music

Appalachian music refers to the folk traditions of the Eastern U.S., specifically the Appalachian mountain range. The music is heavily influenced by the Irish, Scottish, and English emigrants of the eighteenth century and features musical traditions such as English and Scottish ballads, dance tunes, and fiddle songs. African-American musical traditions also contributed to the development of Appalachian music, and conventional aspects of Appalachian folk music, such as the banjo, strong rhythmic drive, harmonic blue notes, and group singing, all originate from African-American slaves of the time. Appalachian music features heavy ornamentation, improvisation, rhythmic and melodic focus, and an upbeat tempo. Typical instruments used in the genre include the banjo, mandolin, guitar, autoharp, American fiddle, fretted dulcimer, dobro, and dulcimer.

Early jazz music

Early jazz music originated from a wide variety of cultural, social, and instrumental influences from the 1890s through the 1910s. New Orleans jazz was one of the earliest forms of jazz music and borrowed from the music of black and creole musicians; it featured frequent interplay between instruments, improvisations, and syncopated march rhythms. Early jazz music, as well as blues music, was heavily influenced by the black church through improvisation, storytelling, call and response, vocal inflections, and the blues progression. Early jazz music also borrowed features of American marching band music and ragtime, such as strong stride rhythms and multi-thematic material. Pianistic harmonies of composers such as Debussy and Ravel also contributed to early jazz music, and composers also incorporated the claves and syncopations of Latin song and dance forms.

Waltz vs. mazurka

Both the waltz and the mazurka were important European dances of the Romantic era and became popular compositional forms in the 1800s. The waltz originated in southern Germany and Austria, while the mazurka originated in the province of Mazovia in Poland. Both dances feature triple time; however, the waltz places emphasis on the downbeat while the mazurka places emphasis on either the second or third beats. Both dances usually consisted of two or four repeated eight-measure sections; however, the waltz eventually evolved to become a longer complex work within art music and included an introduction as well as a coda. The waltz usually held a faster tempo with an elegant style, but stylistic variation among mazurkas was common. Obertas were livelier and more jovial versions; kujawiak were slower and more melancholic forms of the mazurka, while the conventional mazurka typically featured an intense, militant aesthetic.

Importance of Arab culture in the development of North African music

The region of North Africa received considerable cultural influence from the bordering Arabic countries, and the music of North Africa reflects that cultural diversity. The North African region that includes present-day Morocco, Libya, Tunisia, and Algeria is also known by the Arabic term Maghrib ("west"). Although Egypt is geographically included on the African continent, it holds its own unique cultural, musical, and sociopolitical place within North Africa. Arabic-Islamists ruled the Maghrib from approximately the seventh century to the sixteenth century; beginning in the eleventh century, Jewish and Muslim refugees from the al-Andalus region of the Iberian Peninsula brought with them the Arab-

Andalusian music traditions that originated in Baghdad. Elements of Arabic influence in North African music include the Quranic chant, poetry/harp/lute playing, and instruments such as the gimbri, drums, and metal castanets.

West African musical traditions

West Africa holds several local musical traditions such as those used in praise singing, various ceremonies, work activities, and national identities. Court musicians were responsible for continuing the oral tradition through singing and performing several instruments such as the lute, long trumpet, fiddle, and drum. Drum ensembles in south Ghana frequently use bell patterns, but those in Senegal, Niger, and other parts of Ghana use the talking drum, one of the oldest instruments in West Africa. Music plays an important role in birth, adulthood initiations, marriages, and death through singing, drumming, and dancing. During ceremonies, professional musicians perform special music to induce trance, possession, or direct communication with spirits. Praise singing emerged in the twentieth century through the Ghanian musical genre called highlife, which incorporates guitar playing with traditional Akan music.

Djembe

The djembe is a wooden slit drum dating back to the Mali Empire around 1230 AD that can produce a variety of pitches through different hand-striking techniques and drum positions. Typically made of hollowed-out wood, the djembe yields a large sound relative to its size and has been used for speech-like communication. Up until the 1950s, the djembe was only known in its local West African ethnic groups, but has since become popular in Western culture as well. In a traditional African ensemble, multiple drums are used, including a lead djembe and other dunun. Drummers repeat various rhythmic figures resulting in polyrhythms, while the lead djembe accentuates dancers' movements and improvises over the rest of the drumming ensemble. Musicians and singers typically form a circle with the dancers on the inside.

Use of dialogue in African musical form and rhythm

Dialogue, also known as call and response, is an important and unique feature of African musical expression. Within musical aesthetics, dialogue occurs when a musical line "responds" to a previous musical line; this response can come from a different musician, instrument, group, or register within a solo performer. A vocal or instrumental leader might make a call, and another musician or group of musicians might respond with a musical interjection so that phrases are exchanged between the two groups. Solo performers can also have a musical dialogue through musical or extra-musical interjections such as whistles, percussive sounds, or other alternating musical phrases. The call and response form has been an influential African musical element that can be seen in the music of blues, jazz, hip-hop, rock, and gospel.

Traditional African music

Although the continent of Africa holds a great variety of musical expressions, traditions, and instruments among its different regions, certain musical elements remain uniquely African. The call and response form that has so heavily influenced other modern musical genres has been a central feature of African music for centuries. Also distinctive is the use of polyrhythms, syncopation, and offbeat phrasing in rhythmic patterns of the area. Much of African music uses a cyclic form in which various phrases with a set number of beats can be continued as long as the performers want; musicians can begin at any part of the cycle and frequently improvise over the form. Instruments that jingle, buzz, or rattle are also popular in African cultures; examples include the mbira, the dagbamba, and xylophones, lutes, and harps that have been manipulated to buzz, jingle, or rattle when played.

Kabuki

Kabuki is a Japanese theater form stemming from the Edo period of the 1600s that was originally performed by females, but is now performed by males as well. Kesho, the kabuki makeup, is a hallmark of the art form in which a white oshiroi base is decorated with boldly colored kumadori to produce exaggerated and dramatic masks. There are three types of kabuki: jidai-mono are historical plays; sewa-mono are domestic theater dramas; and shosagoto are dance pieces. The form of a kabuki play generally contains four parts: the first part called the deha includes two sections that introduce the mood and ithe characters (oki and michiyuki). The second part called the chuha includes two sections that build the plot emotionally and climactically (kudoki and monogatari). The third part called the odoriji is a dance component. The fourth part called the iriha includes both the musical finale and the end of the plot (chirashi and dangire).

Middle Eastern maqam system of melodic organization

The maqam system of melodic organization used in Middle Eastern music most resembles the Western mode but is distinctively confined to the lower tetra-chord. There are more than 30 different maqamat, and each defines the melodic contour, pitches, and hierarchical development of the scale. The Middle Eastern maqam is not even-tempered as in Western music, as fifth notes are tuned based on the third harmonic; additionally, each of the remaining notes may be tuned differently depending on which maqam is being used. Scalar intervals may include approximations of quartertones, semitones, and even microtones. Musicians frequently compose and improvise over a single maqam but may also modulate to others before returning. Since the nature of the Middle Eastern maqam contains numerous subtle microtonal variations, music of the region is mostly melodic and is rarely ever harmonic.

Traditional Chinese musical instruments

The pipa is a pear-shaped Chinese plucked lute traditionally made with silk thread that has four strings and a bent neck. The pipa has been an important and popular instrument of Chinese culture since the seventh century, and is often played as a solo instrument in performance. The standard tuning for the pipa, A-d-c-a, allows the full chromatic scale to be played. The erhu is another traditional Chinese lute often featured as a solo instrument and has two strings with a bow that sits in between the strings. The traditional instrument is typically made with snakeskin on the sound box and horsehair for the bow. The yangqin is a trapezoidal, hammered dulcimer that is often played solo as well as in ensembles. The dizi is a transverse flute that plays an important role in Chinese folk, operatic, and orchestral music. The instrument includes a special hole in addition to the blowing and finger holes that, when applied, gives the resulting sounds a nasal and buzzing quality.

Australian Aboriginal music

Australian Aboriginal musical instruments include the didgeridoo, the bull-roarer, and the gum leaf. The most well-known of the Aboriginal instruments, the didgeridoo, consists of a simple wooden tube that is slightly flared at the end. Didgeridoo musicians buzz their lips similarly to trumpet players but without a mouthpiece. The sound produced by the didgeridoo is likened to a low-pitched drone and is often used to accompany songs or traditional stories. The bull-roarer consists of a simple wooden slat connected to the end of a length of cord. Sound is produced when the cord is wound and the bull-roarer is whirled in a circular motion. The aerodynamics of this instrument creates a pulsing, low-pitched roar. The gum leaf is a more primitive Aboriginal instrument, yet still plays an important role in the culture and tradition of native Australians. Musicians use the leaf of the Eucalyptus tree, held taut against the lip, as a simple wind valve for the mouth. Skilled players can easily play tunes using the same technique as in whistling.

Music played a key role in Australian Aboriginal culture through storytelling, preserving history, and leading ceremonies. Since there was no formal system of writing, the Aborigines held a strong oral tradition; records were passed down through generations via song and dance. The Aborigines believed that all music comes from the spiritual realm, and new songs were discovered through visions and dreams. Music played an integral role in Aboriginal daily life, and children were encouraged at an early age to sing and dance while doing everyday tasks. The Aborigines had songs that recorded family histories, geographies of the land, rules, and customs. The Aborigines also had secular gossip songs about controversies and relationships. Ceremonial music played an important role in the various spiritual ceremonies, whether to invoke ancestral beings or to purify items of the deceased.

Polynesian nose flute

The nose flute is a widely important wind instrument throughout the Pacific, except for Australia and New Zealand. Commonly made out of bamboo, the nose flute is played through a single nostril, while the other nostril is held shut. Since the nose flute produces a soft and gentle sound, it played an important role in many Polynesian musical traditions. The nose flute was popular during courtship and lovemaking; the timbre and tone of the nose flute had an enticing sound, and as a quiet instrument, encouraged intimacy and privacy for current and prospective lovers. In Tonga, the nose flute was also used as a respectful way to gently awaken the chief of a tribe. Some cultures believed that nose flutes were also instruments that could evoke magical and spiritual qualities.

Inversions of triads and seventh chords

Chords are related by inversion if they contain the same pitches with the same root, but have different pitches sounding in the bass. For triads, a chord is considered to be in root position if the root of the chord is the lowest-sounding pitch. A triad is considered to be in first inversion if the third of the chord is the lowest-sounding pitch. A triad is considered to be in second inversion if the fifth of the chord is the lowest-sounding pitch. For example, the root position triad g-b-d becomes b-d-g' in first inversion and d-g'-b' in second inversion. For seventh chords, the classifications are similar except for the addition of a third inversion, indicating that the seventh of the chord is the lowest-sounding pitch. Thus, for the root position seventh chord g-b-d-f, first inversion becomes b-d-f-g', second inversion becomes d-f-g'-b', and third inversion becomes f-g'-b'-d'.

Authentic cadence

The authentic cadence is defined as a dominant sounding harmony resolving to the tonic harmony, notated as V-I or V-i in Western tonal theory. The authentic cadence is considered to be the strongest cadence because of the presence of the supertonic to tonic progression as well as the leading tone-to-tonic progression. In voice leading, these two progressions exhibit the highest tension and release movements within music theory. An authentic cadence can be either perfect or imperfect. A perfect authentic cadence has both the roots of the V and I chords sounding in the bass, and the tonic as the highest-sounding note on the final chord. An imperfect authentic cadence does not involve all the conditions required to be a perfect authentic cadence, and so may not have the tonic sounding in the highest note of the final chord, or may have inverted chords.

Plagal cadence

The plagal cadence is defined as the subdominant sounding harmony resolving to the tonic harmony, notated as IV-I or iv-i in Western tonal theory. Since there is the absence of a leading tone resolution in a plagal cadence, it is not considered as final or as strong of a cadence as the authentic cadence. Oftentimes, the plagal cadence is found as an extension of an authentic cadence, embellishing the final tonic through the neighboring notes of the third and fourth scale degrees, and of the fifth and sixth scale degrees. The plagal cadence is a common ending to many Protestant hymns, and is also known as the amen cadence, as the cadence is set to the word amen. The plagal cadence is so closely associated with Protestant hymns that some composers have used the IV-I progression as an allusion to its sacred usage.

Deceptive cadence

The deceptive cadence is defined as the dominant-sounding harmony progressing to a harmony that defies the expected tonic harmony, most commonly the submediant harmony. The leading tone of the dominant resolves to the tonic of the key, but the tonic pitch acts as either the third or fifth of the chord, instead of the root. The dominant chord in deceptive cadences can progress to the submediant harmony, notated as V-VI or V-vi, or to the subdominant harmony, notated as V-IV or V-iv. The deceptive cadence is an important compositional tool in avoiding an ending, and is useful not only in delaying or prolonging an ending, but also in transitioning to another structural section of music. This cadence is considered to be a weak cadence, as there is little to no sense of resolution in the music. Another name for the deceptive cadence is the interrupted cadence.

Half cadence

The half cadence is defined as any harmony progressing to a dominant harmony. The preceding harmony can be the tonic, subdominant, supertonic, or any other harmony. A common half cadence is the tonic in second inversion resolving to the dominant, notated as I64 - - V in Western tonal theory. This particular half cadence is known as the cadential tonic six-four, and shares the bass note from the six-four chord with the resulting dominant chord. Oftentimes, the cadential tonic six-four progression occurs at the end of the first section in a two-part or binary piece of music. Other types of half cadences include the Phrygian half cadence, in which a first inversion subdominant chord proceeds to the dominant similarly in the Phrygian mode, and the Lydian half cadence, in which a first inversion subdominant chord is raised by a half step and then resolved to the dominant.

Imperfect and perfect cadences

The terms imperfect and perfect cadences apply to the authentic and plagal cadences. An authentic or plagal cadence classifies as perfect if both of the chords are in root position and the tonic pitch sounds in the highest voice. An authentic or plagal cadence classifies as imperfect if either of the chords are in an inversion and/or the tonic pitch does not sound in the highest voice. An example of a perfect authentic cadence is the progression V-I with the tonic of the last chord sounding in the highest voice. An example of an imperfect authentic cadence is the progression V6-I. An example of a perfect plagal cadence is the progression IV-I with the tonic of the last chord sounding in the highest voice. An example of an imperfect plagal cadence is the IV-I progression in which the last chord does not contain the tonic in the highest-sounding voice.

Scale degrees

A scale degree is an assigned number to the sequential notes of any major or minor scale. Since the Western tonal language is transposable in all keys, this systematic approach to music theory aids comprehensive musical analysis. The pitches of any major or minor scale are numbered 1-7, usually indicated in upper-case Roman numerals for major harmonies and lower-case Roman numerals for minor harmonies as follows: I, ii, iii, IV, V, vi, and viio. Each scale degree is also given a label so that I is the tonic, II is the supertonic, III is the mediant, IV is the subdominant, V is the dominant, VI is the submediant, and VII is the leading tone or the subtonic. The scale degrees in Western tonal music function similarly in the diatonic scale, and conventions can be generalized, such as the stable importance of the tonic or the tendency for the leading tone to progress to the tonic.

Circle of fifths

The circle of fifths describes the relationship and pattern of major and minor keys from one to the next as they move up or down in fifths. Moving up a fifth from C becomes G; moving up a fifth from G becomes D; and moving up a fifth from D becomes A, etc. The circle of fifths is modeled so that eventually, with enharmonic naming, it goes through all 12 keys back to C. As each key moves along the circle, a sharp or flat is added depending on the direction of the circle. For example, the key of C major has zero flats; moving down a fifth, F major has one flat; moving down another fifth, Bb has two flats, etc. The circle of fifths can be applied to both major keys and to minor keys, and is also useful in determining the degree of relatedness among keys.

Natural, melodic, and harmonic minors

In Western tonal theory, the minor scale is the following pattern of whole and half steps: whole-half-whole-whole-half-whole-whole. The minor scale is similar to the Aeolian mode of the Renaissance era. This minor scale without alterations is termed the natural minor scale, or the pure minor scale. If the minor scale is altered so that the seventh note of the scale is raised by a half step, then it is termed the harmonic minor scale. If the minor scale is altered so that both the sixth and the seventh notes of the scale are raised by a half step in ascending motion, and lowered to the natural minor in descending motion, then the scale is termed melodic minor scale. These patterns can be applied to any of the 12 pitches to produce the natural, melodic, and harmonic minor scales.

Whole tone scale and the chromatic scale

The whole tone scale is a scale in which every pitch is separated by a whole step. Within Western musical tonality, there are two different whole tone scales, each made up of six pitches. The whole tone scale can be either C-D-E-F#-G#-A# or C#-D#-F-G-A-B. The chromatic scale, on the other hand, is a scale in which every pitch is separated by a half step. Within Western musical tonality, the chromatic scale includes all 12 pitches of an octave. Both the whole tone scale and the chromatic scale lack a clear tonal center, as either of the scales could start on any key without any definite hierarchy to the pattern. However, composers tend to use the chromatic scale as a tool to increase complexity, while the whole tone scale is a useful tool to give a feeling of vague spaciousness.

12-tone music

Twelve-tone music is a system of musical theory in which a composition is based on a serial ordering of all 12 pitches that stipulates the sequence in which those 12 pitches should appear in the composition. The 12-tone system of music arose as a result of the growing disdain for traditional tonal music. This theory of composition became a way for music to be planned in an abstract manner, into a serial row that establishes the pitch structure of the resulting composition. Rows can be manipulated throughout the composition through retrograde, inversion, or retrograde-inversion. The rows can also be transposed to start on a different pitch wherein the same intervallic relationship of the row is kept intact. Arnold Schoenberg, a leading Austrian composer of the Second Viennese School, began to develop this theory of composition in the early 1920s and continued to compose 12-tone music throughout the twentieth century.

Tonal vs. real answer to a fugal subject

The fugue is a form of imitative counterpoint in which a fugue theme is introduced at the beginning of the work, also known as the exposition, and is echoed in all of the fugal voices though imitation and development. The term fugue comes from the Latin fugere meaning "to flee," as each voice essentially chases the previous voice. The initial subject is called the leader, or dux, and is presented in the tonic key. The dux is usually followed by the comes, the companion answer in the dominant key, which can be presented in one of two ways: real or tonal. In a real answer to a fugal subject, the theme is transposed exactly note to note in the dominant key. In a tonal answer to a fugal subject, the theme is transposed loosely in the dominant key, modified so as to maintain harmonic congruity or to facilitate modulations.

Tone cluster

A tone cluster is a group of closely spaced notes played simultaneously, usually in intervals of adjacent seconds and groupings, or "clusters." The term usually refers to stacks of more than two neighboring notes, with three being the minimum. Tone clusters can be diatonic, chromatic, and dia-chromatic. For diatonic tone clusters, only neighboring notes in the diatonic key are used. For chromatic tone clusters, notes that are separated by a half-step are used. For dia-chromatic tone clusters, both diatonic seconds and chromatic notes are used. Tone clusters appeared rarely in music before the 1900s, and were not considered a definite compositional tool until the 1900s. The concept of "tone cluster" was termed by the American composer Henry Cowell (1897-1965) in the 1920s, and appears in compositions by Western classical composers such as Charles Ives, Béla Bartók, Lou Harrison, Henry Cowell, Olivier Messiaen, Karlheinz Stockhausen, and George Crumb, as well as in jazz and popular music.

Italian tempo markings

The tempo marking adagio comes from the Italian ad agio meaning, "at ease," and is understood to mean a slower tempo than andante, but faster than largo. The tempo marking moderato means "moderately" in Italian, and is a relative tempo designation that is faster than andante, but slower than allegro. The tempo marking presto means "very fast" in Italian, and is generally treated as a very quick tempo, much faster than allegro, and if prestissimo, then as fast as possible. The tempo marking andante means "at a walking pace" in Italian, and is a more ambiguous tempo that can be thought of as faster than adagio but slower than allegro. The tempo marking allegro means "lively, merry" in Italian, and is generally treated as a fast or moderately fast tempo.

Hemiola

The term hemiola comes from the Greek meaning "one and a half," also known as the ratio of three to two. Its use in ancient Greek and Latin musical theory referred to the interval of the fifth, as the fifth is made up of two strings with lengths of 3:2. The term hemiola also refers to the rhythm of three notes in a space that usually only has two notes, whether in succession or simultaneously. Horizontal hemiola, or a hemiola in succession, refers to a change in note values where, for example, three quarter notes follow a measure of two dotted half notes in 6/4 meter. Vertical hemiola, or a hemiola that occurs simultaneously, refers to a rhythmic syncopation where, for example, three quarter notes play over two dotted quarter notes in 6/8 meter. However, music theorists prefer to use the Latin term sesquialtera in cases of vertical hemiola as a more accurate representation of the three-against-two rhythm.

Metrical accenting

Metrical accenting refers to the natural stresses on certain beats of a meter. This can be defined by the meter itself or by the style or origin of the musical rhythm. In a simple 3/4 meter, the tendency for a metrical accent falls on the first beat of the measure. However, in certain musical styles, such as the Polish mazurka and other folk dances, the metrical stress may be on the second beat in 3/4 meter. In 4/4 meter, there is naturally a primary stress on the downbeat of the measure, and a secondary, weaker stress on the third beat of the measure. However, in certain jazz and world music, the accents may be on the second and fourth beats for stylistic accuracy. In compound meters such as 6/8, 9/8, and 12/8 time, there is a natural accent on the first of every group of three eighth notes.

Compound vs. simple meters

In both simple and compound meters, the numbers in the meter refer to the subdivision of beats within a musical measure. The number on the top, also known as the numerator, specifies the number of pulses or beats in a measure. The number on the bottom, also known as the denominator, specifies which note-value gets a pulse. For example, in 2/4 meter, there are two beats per measure, with the quarter note receiving each pulse. Simple meters cannot be subdivided into smaller groups and include meters such as 2/4, 4/4, 2/2, 4/2, 5/4, and 3/4. In a compound meter, the number of pulses can be subdivided into groups of three. For example, 6/8 meter has six pulses per measure with the eighth note receiving the pulse, and is thus a compound meter. Other examples of compound meters include 9/8 and 12/8 meters.

Binary vs. rounded binary form

Binary form refers to the structure of a musical composition with regard to thematic, tonal, dynamic, and textural structure. Binary form consists of two main sections, both repeated. The first section, labeled A, presents the tonic key of the composition. The second section, A', is often labeled B but is more precisely a modified version of A; the musical material of A' is often in the dominant key if the tonic was major, or in the relative major key if the tonic was minor. Simple binary form is considered to be an open form, as neither A nor A' can exist independently. In a rounded binary form, there is a return to the original thematic material of A. Thus, the form can be represented as ABA or AA'A. The initial A section as well as the A' (or B) – A section are both repeated as in simple binary form and should not be confused with ternary form.

Ternary form

Ternary form refers to the structure of a musical composition with regard to thematic, tonal, dynamic, and textural structure. Ternary form consists of three main sections in which the first and third sections are nearly identical with a contrasting second section. The first section, labeled A, presents the tonic key of the composition, and returns at the end of the composition in the third section, also labeled A. The middle section, labeled B, is usually in a related key and cadences in the same key or another closely related key before the third section begins. The form can be represented as ABA; in ternary form, sections are not repeated as in a rounded binary form, and the middle section is usually distinctly different: B instead of A'. Ternary form is considered to be a closed form, since all three sections could exist independently.

Monophy, homophony, polyphony, and heterophony

The term monophy refers to the texture of any music that is made up of a single melodic line. The melodic line can be performed by a solo musician or by a group of musicians. Examples include plainchant, minnesinger, Meistersinger, and troubadour music. The term homophony refers to the texture of any music that is made up of a main melodic line over a supporting accompaniment. Examples include most rock, pop, country, and jazz music. The term polyphony refers to the texture of any music that is made up of many equally important melodic lines. Examples include much of Renaissance and Baroque music. The term heterophony refers to the texture of any music that is made up of multiple improvised interpretations of the same melody played at the same time. Heterophony mostly occurs in non-Western music cultures such as those of East Asia, South Asia, Southeast Asia, and the Middle East.

Equal- and unequal-voice polyphony

The term polyphony refers to the texture of any music that is made up of many equally important melodic lines. Examples include much of Renaissance and Baroque music. Within polyphony, there exists equal- and unequal-voice polyphony. Equal-voice polyphony refers to polyphony that maintains the same thematic material in all the individual voices. A prime example of equal-voice polyphony is the canon, in which the exact same melodic material enters sequentially after a uniform time interval. Other examples of equal-voice polyphony include fugues, inventions, and other forms of imitation. Unequal-voice polyphony refers to polyphony in which greater importance is given to one or more melodic lines. Examples of unequal-voice polyphony include Medieval-era cantus firmus compositions that give musical precedence to the cantus firmus, usually sung or played in the tenor voice.

Contrary motion, parallel motion, similar motion, and oblique motion

Contrary motion, parallel motion, similar motion, and oblique motion all refer to the simultaneous movement of two or more musical lines. The terms can describe both vocal and instrumental musical lines moving in parts at the same time. Contrary motion refers to the motion of two musical lines that move in opposite directions. Parallel motion refers to the motion of two musical lines that move in the same direction, whether upwards or downwards, while maintaining the same interval between the lines. Similar motion refers to the motion of two musical lines that move in similar directions, whether upwards or downwards, but without maintaining the same interval between the lines. Oblique motion refers to the motion of two musical lines in which one line stays stationary while the other musical line moves in an upward or downward direction.

Types of dissonance found in tonal counterpoint

In tonal counterpoint, careful regulations have been made to avoid dissonances; however, certain types of dissonances are allowed, in the form of voice-leading treatments. If an anticipation tone is dissonant yet unaccented, it is allowed if it is then directly reharmonized. Dissonance is also allowed in the cambiata, a figure that usually moves down a second to a dissonant pitch, down another third to a consonant pitch, then up a second that can be dissonant or consonant. Another form of allowable dissonance is the appoggiatura, in which there is a leap to a dissonance followed by a descending step. Also allowed is a suspension, in which a dissonance tone sounds on a downbeat and is then resolved downward by step. A passing tone moves in a stepwise motion through two consonant tones. A neighbor tone also moves in a stepwise motion but returns to the original consonant tone. An escape tone is a dissonant note that is approached by step and resolved by a leap in the opposite direction.

Interval types

Intervals measure the semitones, or half-steps, between any two tones in Western music theory; additional information can be applied through five descriptive adjectives: perfect, major, minor, diminished, and augmented. A perfect interval only refers to the unison, fourth, fifth, and octave; when any perfect interval is lowered by a half-step, it becomes a diminished interval. When any perfect interval is raised by a half-step, it becomes an augmented interval. Major intervals can refer to the second, third, sixth, and seventh intervals. Major intervals occur in a diatonic major scale and measure the relationships between those two pitches. When any major interval is lowered by a half-step, it becomes a minor interval. When any minor interval is lowered by a half-step, it becomes a diminished interval. When any major interval is raised by a half-step, it becomes an augmented interval.

Relative minor vs. parallel minor

For any diatonic major scale, there exists a relative minor and parallel minor of that scale. The relative minor scale shares the same key signature as the major scale. The parallel minor scale shares only the same tonic pitch. F major, for example, has the relative minor scale of d minor, which shares the same key signature of one flat, and the parallel minor scale of f minor, which shares the same tonic pitch of F. Both the relative minor and the parallel minor scales are frequently used as common keys to modulate to within a composition. In the relative minor, composers can easily modulate to a relative minor by using any of the shared chords, since the key signature is identical for the relative major and minor keys. Parallel minor keys offer the same dominant chord as the parallel major key, but have less in common, since the key signatures of parallel major and minor chords are unrelated.

Clefs commonly used in orchestral writing

The four main clefs commonly used in orchestral writing are the treble, alto, tenor, and bass clefs. The treble clef, also known as the G-clef, is shaped so that the spiral of the symbol circles the G-line on the staff. The instruments that typically employ the treble clef include the violin, woodwinds, high basses, and the treble range of keyboard instruments. The alto clef, also known as the C-clef, is shaped so that the middle point of the symbol rests on the third line as middle C. The instrument that typically employs the alto clef is the viola. The tenor clef also uses the C-clef, but is placed so that the middle point of the symbol rests on the fourth line as middle C. Instruments that sometimes use the tenor clef include the cello, bassoon, and trombone. The bass clef, also known as the F-clef, is shaped so that two dots of the symbol surround the F-line. Instruments that typically employ the bass clef include the double bass, cello, bassoon, trombone, low brasses, and the bass range of keyboard instruments.

Concert band instruments vs. symphonic band instruments

Both concert bands and symphonic bands employ a wide range of instruments that include the brass family, the woodwind family, and the percussion family, as well as a wide variety of timbres, colors, and ranges. The concert band focuses on popular band music and orchestral transcriptions, while the symphonic band is more comparable to a symphonic orchestra in range. The concert band has prescribed parts for two flutes, two oboes, two bassoons, three clarinets, one bass clarinet, four saxophones, four horns, three trumpets, three trombones, one baritone horn, one tuba, and three or four percussion instruments, with a total of 40-50 performers. The symphonic band tends to have larger sections with a total of 90-120 performers, and may include the string bass, piccolo, English horn, harp, bass trombone, contrabassoon, and/or a saxophone.

Conventional parts of four-part harmony

In four-part harmony, the conventional parts from high to low are soprano, alto, tenor, and bass. The general vocal range of the soprano voice is from c', middle C, to a''. The general vocal range of the alto voice is from F to d''. The general vocal range of the tenor voice is from B to g'. The general vocal range of the bass clef is from E to c'. Other vocal parts include the baritone and the mezzo-soprano; the general vocal range of the baritone is from G to e', and the general range of the mezzo-soprano is from A to f'. Although many composers use these ranges in writing a piece of four-part harmony, the voice as an instrument remains one of the most complex of instruments, as each individual's voice can vary drastically in range and ability.

Standard instrumentation of the concert band

The standard instrumentation of the concert band as prescribed by members of the American Band Association helped to cultivate the concert band as an essential performing ensemble in American musical culture. With the standardization of concert band instrumentation in the early twentieth century, publishers Boosey and Company, and Chappell, helped to grow the repertoire of concert bands, especially for the school and community settings. The American Band Association prescribed the concert band as having parts for two flutes, two oboes, two bassoons, three clarinets, one bass clarinet, four saxophones, four horns, three trumpets, three trombones, one baritone horn, one tuba, and three or four percussion instruments, with a total of 40-50 performers.

Classical orchestra instrument families

In the Classical era, music became highly homophonic with a focus on melody and accompaniment textural form. To accommodate for the change in compositional form, the Classical orchestra shifted the way it used certain instrument families. In the Baroque era, strings and winds were often doubled to play certain lines. With the advent of melodic authority, first violins were now the dominant string section while the lower strings became the supporting background harmonically and rhythmically. Wind parts were simplified from the Baroque contrapuntal lines and were now supporting background harmonies as well. As the Classical era progressed, Mozart eventually restored the wind section's melodic role within the orchestra. During the Classical era, the bassoon became increasingly independent, as opposed to the previous Baroque setting of the bassoon as part of the bass line. Brass also began to be used in a greater independent capacity during the Classical period.

How pitches are defined

All clefs indicate the position of a particular pitch on the five-lined staff. The G-clef, the C-clef, and the F-clef are the most common clefs used in modern Western music notation. The G-clef spirals around the second line from the bottom, indicating it as the G line for the G pitch above middle C. The C-clef has a middle point that is placed to indicate the line as middle C. The C-clef can be placed on the third line, which is typically called the alto or viola clef; when it is placed on the fourth line from the bottom, it is typically called the tenor clef. The F-clef looks somewhat like a backwards C with two dots to the right of it; the top point of the curve is placed on the fourth line from the bottom so that the two dots also surround the same line, indicating it as the F pitch below middle C.

Role of notes, rests, and time signatures

Rhythm is the movement of music over time. As such, certain musical aspects such as pitch duration, silence, and meter play key roles in translating musical symbols to real-time musical rhythm. Pitch durations are notated through note values that sound for a specified time. Whole notes are held through four quarter-note lengths. Half notes are held through two quarter-note lengths. Quarter notes are held for half the length of a half note. Eighth notes are held for half the length of a quarter note. Sixteenth notes are held for half the length of an eighth note, and so forth. Silence durations are notated through rests, which have note name equivalents, i.e., whole notes and whole rests both have durations of four quarter-note lengths. Meters are essential in establishing rhythm, as meters define the general organization of stresses and pulses.

Durational rhythm vs. tonal rhythm

A preliminary study (Schachter 1976) put forward that musical rhythm arises through two separate sources, leading to what Schachter calls tonal rhythm and durational rhythm. Durational rhythm is closely tied with meter, and consists of the aspect of rhythm associated with patterns of durations, emphases, and groupings. In contrast, tonal rhythm does not arise from patterns of stress and duration, and is essentially independent of meter. It instead arises from rhythmic properties of the tonal system. Example sources of tonal rhythm include recurrence of a single tone, the octave relationship, chordal and linear associations, consonances, and dissonances. It is important to note that any series of tones will have rhythmic characteristics that will be defined by the relative structural importance of the tones, and that duration and structural importance may be unrelated.

Bowing techniques

The détaché bowing technique requires the player to detach the notes by playing one note per bow stroke. The ondulé technique describes a bow stroke in which the bow plays two adjacent strings like a tremolo. Sautillé describes the bouncing of the notes by the middle of the bow that is typically played at a fast tempo. Sul ponticello refers to the use of the bow close to the bridge in which a harsh grating sound is produced. Sul tasto refers to the use of the bow over the end of the fingerboard to produce a light airy sound. Martelé refers to the abrupt release of a stroke in a forceful manner. Ricochet refers to the rapid bouncing of the upper third of the bow as the player drops the bow on a down-bow. Louré refers to the slight detachment of the notes without changing the direction of the bow. Col legno refers to using the stick of the bow on the strings instead of the hair.

Cadenza in the eighteenth and nineteenth centuries

A cadenza is described as a section in a large concerto or ensemble work in which the soloist plays without any accompanying instruments. The cadenza may be improvised or written out, but usually occurs at the end of a prominent cadence such as the ending tonic cadence of a movement. The accompanying instruments may pause or play a sustaining note while the soloist continues with the cadenza. In the eighteenth and nineteenth centuries, cadenzas became increasingly virtuosic and included more thematic material from the work. Although still commonly improvised as from early times, cadenzas were also increasingly written out by composers as they integrated more complex and elaborate material. Many cadenzas became prescribed instead of merely optional, and were also placed in increasingly unconventional places within the musical work.

Importance of vocal timbre in characterizing different emotions

In vocal performance, it is important to express the emotion or mood of the music through timbre. Just as vocal expression communicates emotion through regular speech, in music, vocal qualities and inflections help to communicate emotion to the listening audience. As in speech, to communicate emotions like disgust and loathing, the singer uses a darker timbral quality and may include a raspy delivery and harsher consonants. To communicate emotions like hope and assurance, the singer uses a brighter timbral quality with a smooth, flowing delivery. To communicate emotions like sorrow and gloom, the singer uses a dark and hollow timbral quality and may include a shaky delivery as in regular speech. To communicate emotions like anger and vengeance, the singer uses an intensified dark timbral quality with sonorous delivery of vowels and consonants.

Music terms

The dynamic markings forzando (z), rinforzando (rinf), and sforzando (sfz) all refer to an increased loudness in sound. All three Italian directives have roots from the Italian word forzare, which means "to force." Forzando, meaning forced, directs the musician to strongly accent the notes over which the marking occurs. Rinforzando, however, has an added prefix and means more precisely "reinforcing" or "strengthening." The Rinf. dynamic marking usually refers to the increase in volume of a group of notes throughout a phrase and is played increasingly louder similarly to a cresc. but over a shorter length of time. Sforzando is most similar to forzando, and the two terms can be interchanged to mean a sudden increase in loudness of the note or notes over which the marking occurs.

Con, "with," indicates each of these terms as descriptions or instructions of a performer's phrasing. Con amore translates to "with love," and is equivalent to amorevole or amoroso, "lovingly." Con amore may have multiple correlates within the performance style, translating into a legato articulation, rubato, and more dramatic dynamic contrast. Con bravura, similarly, translates to "with bravery" and is a different connotation from bravura as in a bravura performance, which means "skill." Con brio, or brioso, "with spirit"; con fuoco, "with fire"; con grazia "with grace"; con tenerezza, "with tenderness." Each term is somewhat subjective; indeed, it may be difficult to establish a clear distinction between con amore, con tenerezza, and con grazia, for example, and will result in similar interpretations. Con brioso, con fuoco, and con bravura also have many characteristics in common and will differ from an amoroso performance that would have more staccato articulations and limited rubato.

Articulation markings can range from those indicating a shortening of pitch duration to those indicating a lengthening of pitch duration. These articulation markings are presented in decreasing order of duration length: tenuto, portato, staccato, and staccatissimo. Tenuto, from the Italian word tenere meaning "to hold," directs the player to hold the note for its full value. In musical notation, a horizontal line over or under the note head marks the tenuto. Portato, from the Italian word portare meaning "to carry," directs the player to smoothly detach the notes similarly to a legato, but shorter in length and longer than a staccato. Both dots and a slur over or under the note heads mark the portato. Staccato, from the Italian word staccare meaning "to detach," directs the player to shortly detach the note. A dot over or under the note head marks the staccato. Staccatissimo is an extremely shortened note and is notated by a wedge or pike above or under the note head.

These tempo markings in order from slowest to fastest are: larghissimo, largo, larghetto, andante, moderato, allegro, vivace, and presto. Larghissimo comes from the Italian meaning "very or extremely broad" and should be played very slowly. Largo comes from the Italian meaning "broad" and should be played slowly. Larghetto is slightly faster than largo. Andante comes from the Italian meaning "in a walking manner" and should be played slightly faster than adagio, but slower than moderato. Moderato comes from the Italian meaning "moderately" and should be played at an easy comfortable pace. Allegro comes from the Italian meaning "fast" and should be played at a quick tempo. Vivace comes from the Italian meaning "lively" and should be played faster than allegro but slower than presto. Presto comes from the Italian meaning "very fast" and should be played very quickly.

The terms affretando, slentando, allargando, and calando all direct the musician to produce a change in tempo. Affretando comes from the Italian word affretare, which means "to hurry." When notated within musical notation, affretando indicates a quickening of the tempo and also a character or mood of agitation. Slentando means comes from the Italian word slentare, which means "to slow down." The player should gradually decrease the tempo of the section as the music slows down. Allargando comes from the Italian word allargare, which means "to widen." In music, the player should gradually decrease the tempo in a deliberate and imposing character. Calando comes from the Italian word calare, which means "to let down." Musically, the player should gradually decrease both the tempo and the volume, as calando indicates a mood of calming and dying away.

Curricula and Instructional Planning

Selecting music for an ensemble

For any conductor, it is his or her final responsibility to select appropriate music for an ensemble. The conductor should consider the ability level of the ensemble; music should not be impossibly hard or too easy, but just challenging enough for the ensemble to be able to play the music as well as to progress musically and technically. The conductor should also consider the strengths and weaknesses of the ensemble. The music should not always cater to an ensemble's strengths, but should also help to develop any weaknesses an ensemble may have. The conductor should also consider the number of players and instruments in the ensemble; minor changes can be made, but it is difficult to rearrange a full instrumentation to a few instruments. When selecting music, the conductor should also take into account the number of rehearsals before the given performance; there should be adequate time to rehearse any given piece. The conductor should also select a variety of music appropriate for the audience and occasion of the performance.

Full ensemble rehearsal

In a regular full ensemble rehearsal, the conductor or director should prepare a comprehensive plan for the time with the ensemble. Since rehearsal time is usually limited, the conductor should prioritize the musical goals for the session beforehand. The sequencing of the rehearsal goals is up to the conductor, based on the musical works and ensemble, but every rehearsal should have these general components. In the beginning, the ensemble should spend adequate time warming up their instruments and bodies as well as tuning their instruments. This practice helps to develop both the musician's habits as well as listening with awareness. The ensemble should have time with the conducting and playing of various musical works. The ensemble should also spend time refining technically and musically challenging sections. There should also be time for the musicians to develop musicality and sight-reading during the rehearsal.

Sectional rehearsals

Sectional rehearsals are an important tool for the rehearsing ensemble. When too much time is spent on an individual section or part during the full ensemble rehearsal, time is wasted and musicians can become unengaged. Sectional rehearsals allow players to fine-tune their parts together and to fix any technical or musical problems apart from the full ensemble. Sometimes the conductor may not be aware of other hidden problems except through listening to sectional rehearsals. However, certain precautions should be taken to ensure the highest efficiency of a sectional rehearsal. Sectionals should be scheduled either immediately before or after a full ensemble rehearsal; that way, the progress made through a sectional can be immediately integrated within the full ensemble for the most improvement. Players should also be aware of clear objectives before beginning any sectional to avoid wasting time within a sectional.

Individual student lessons

For any student in a large group ensemble, there can be many benefits for the student in taking additional individual lessons with a private teacher. Although a student can learn the basics solely through ensemble rehearsals, it is preferable for students to learn the basics with the help of a private teacher. In an ensemble rehearsal, the conductor can only give so much attention to an individual student, as there are many other students who may need help as well. With a private teacher, the student can have undivided help from a focused professional to guide the student's musical education, ensuring that proper technique and musicality are reinforced from the beginning. As the student progresses to a more advanced level, having a private teacher will better assist in technical challenges and fingering issues that cannot be addressed as easily in a large group ensemble. With a private teacher, a student can advance more quickly to a higher level of playing.

Rhythm

In a full elementary class, there are many important instructional strategies to effectively teach rhythm to young students. The students must first experience rhythm; this can be achieved through kinesthetic movement, whether by clapping, swaying the body, or dancing. The music educator can have students mimic certain clapping or dancing patterns so that the students experience the rhythms before labeling the rhythms. Students can also experience rhythms by keeping a beat to music, to help feel for a steady beat. The music educator can refer to a steady beat as a heartbeat, relating it to a familiar internal process. Once students have experienced certain rhythms, the music educator can begin to assign visual and verbal labels to the rhythms. The association between label and rhythms can thus be strengthened, as the students already know the rhythms through experience.

Student behavior issues

When teaching a group of more than 15 students, certain strategies will benefit the educational environment. If there are instructions, they should clear and concise. When students understand instructions for a task, they are more likely to stay focused and on task. Follow the instructions with reinforcement by modeling the activity, asking the students to repeat the instructions back, or having the students do an example of the activity together, to ensure that students understand and can proceed with the activity. If instructions are not made clear, problems such as student frustration or loss of group control could occur. In addition, always establish rules, awards, and consequences for the classroom. It is essential that students have guidelines to operate within, so that when behavior issues do arise, the educator can act simply and according to guidelines rather than out of emotion.

Keeping students focused

Keeping students focused and on task is one way to prevent behavior issues. There are many instructional strategies to refocus a misbehaving student. If students are distracted, wait until they are paying attention to continue the lesson. Silence will draw attention to the misbehaving students. If students are distracted, educators can redirect their attention by giving a direction such as "If you hear my voice, clap once." (Teachers may need to continue with clap twice, three times, etc.) Misbehaving students will redirect their attention and try not to be left out. Teachers can also reward good behavior through positive reinforcement. If needed, students should be separated. Establish a quieting signal such as raising a hand, or two fingers. Teachers can also place a misbehaving student next to them so that the student becomes conscious of his or her behavior among his classmates. Another technique is to give the misbehaving student a special task; oftentimes, a distracted student is one who is not challenged by the current lesson. Finally, if students continue misbehaving, the teacher may be talking too much, so adjustments may be needed to keep the students actively focused and involved.

Curriculum and objectives

In grades 1-2, students experience a wider range of musical characteristics, learning more about music by doing. Students should follow a balanced curriculum that includes experiential learning such as playing, singing, and moving to music. In a sample six-week curriculum that focuses on introducing rhythm to students, the first week might include games and songs that introduce the concept of a steady beat to students. In the second week, the concept of a steady beat should be reinforced while associating certain beats with certain counts (i.e., quarter note = 1 count, half note = 2 counts). In the third week, steady beat and notes should be reinforced through movement and songs. In the fourth week, the students should compose rhythms of quarter and half notes to music. In the fifth and sixth weeks, students should continue to reinforce these concepts as well as improvise on the learned rhythms through games, dance, and songs.

Students in grades 5-8 should be reinforcing skills acquired in grades K-4, while preparing to achieve the standards set by the National Achievement Standards by grade 8. Students should be able to sing with expression from a variety of styles and genres by memory, on pitch, alone as well as in groups. Students should be able to perform on at least one instrument alone as well as in groups with good technique, posture, bowing or breath, and with good fingering. Students should be able to play simple tunes by ear. Students should also be able to improvise short melodies and simple accompaniment patterns. Students should be able to compose simple compositions in a variety of styles. Students should be able to read treble and bass clefs, and whole, half, quarter, eighth, and sixteenth notes and rests in a variety of meters. Students should be able to analyze basic meter, rhythm, intervals, chords, and tonality. Students should also be able to relate music to history, other arts, and disciplines outside of music.

Affects of physical, cognitive, and social development on music learning

As students progress through puberty in ages 10-14 for girls and 12-16 for boys, there are many changes physically, cognitively, and socially that affect their music learning. Students will be going through many growth spurts, and their reference for posture or instrument positioning may need to be adjusted accordingly. Also, voice development will affect vocal students as the larynx enlarges and the vocal chords lengthen and thicken. The physiological changes of the vocal mechanisms tend to affect boys more than girls, evident in the "cracking" of the voice. During puberty, students will have to work towards singing voice production, pitch accuracy, increasing vocal range, and maintaining a positive attitude towards choral singing. Cognitively, students in puberty are increasingly able to process conceptual ideas and should work on self-regulating musical activities and performances. Socially, students in puberty tend to need more opportunities for self-expression, autonomy, and acceptance in their music learning.

Sequencing a music curriculum

Principles of sequencing a music curriculum can be based on three different techniques: content sequencing, task sequencing, or sequencing of elaboration. When sequencing based on content, the instructor should analyze the content for the main item and then organize the general content into a hierarchal structure. The most general and inclusive content should be presented first, leading the way to more detailed ideas while all the while relating them to former learning content. When sequencing based on a task, the instructor should analyze the skill involved and order the learning progression from simple, more elementary tasks towards more complex skills that build on previous tasks. When sequencing based on elaboration, the students are given an overall view of the knowledge, and then presented with basic content first, progressing towards more detailed information while keeping the organizing overall theme in place.

Aural learners

Students whose primary learning style is that of aural learning need specific teaching techniques to help them succeed. Aural learners learn best by hearing educational content, so teachers should frequently use precise terms when explaining an idea. Aural learners also learn through talking and discussion, so a useful teaching technique is allowing students to discuss ideas and content among themselves. Aural learners may need to question and talk through ideas to help thoroughly comprehend educational content, so teachers should not brush off students' questions, but allow ample time for student questions and answers. Another technique to accommodate aural learners, who need to hear ideas and talk through them, is to have spoken quizzes and tests, to allow aural learners the opportunity to talk through a concept. A helpful technique particularly for aural music learners is to listen to a recording of one's own rehearsals to be able to hear for mistakes and areas for improvement.

Visual learners

Students whose primary learning style is that of visual learning need specific teaching techniques to help them succeed. Visual learners learn best by seeing educational content. When teachers are explaining educational content or instructions, they should also provide a visual explanation, either through a projector or handouts, or by demonstrating the concepts visually. Educators can also encourage visual learners to make flashcards, a helpful tool to visually learn content. Another practical tool for visual learners are pictures, diagrams, and concept maps. These all allow students to visually integrate the learning content internally. When demonstrating instrumental technique or posture, the educator should make sure that all students can see, to accommodate for those who are also visual learners. Without a visual model, visual learners will have a harder time assimilating the new concepts and skills.

Kinesthetic learners

Students whose primary learning style is that of kinesthetic learning need specific teaching techniques to help them succeed. Kinesthetic learners learn best by doing, and need to integrate movement with the introduction of new educational concepts and ideas. Music educators should implement teaching techniques that require students to move while learning new educational content. Lesson segments should be kept short with frequent breaks to stand up and move. When introducing concepts such as rhythm and meter, the music educator should require students to physically move to the various rhythms and meters to accommodate those who are kinesthetic learners. When teaching specific instrumental techniques, the instructor should make sure that the kinesthetic learner demonstrates the movement or technique, rather than merely verbally or visually explaining the concept. Educators can also implement frequent games, field trips, and seating changes.

The kinesthetic theories of rhythm reading hold that rhythm cannot be experienced without having first experienced its movement physically. Since rhythm refers to the flow of movement through space, students should experience rhythm through their bodies first. Once the rhythm has been experienced physically through movement, students will more readily be able to audiate the rhythm mentally during rhythm reading. Phyllis Weikart, a prominent figure in movement pedagogy, advocated the introduction of movement-based learning in early childhood education, so that early gross motor development could better prepare students for more complex rhythmic integration in musical development. Other motor theorists also found that rudimentary motor movements are formed before the age of five, and all other motor movements after the age of five are reinforcements and stabilizations of those fundamental motor movements learned in early childhood.

Accommodations in the music classroom

When a music classroom is able to accommodate students with physical disabilities, there are numerous benefits for both the disabled students as well as the average student. Inclusion promotes social awareness and acceptance, increased motor development, and higher mental acuity. Music educators can accommodate students with physical disabilities in a number of ways. The music classroom should be ADA-accessible and free from obstacles or other hazards. Also, the instructor can acquire adaptive instruments that allow students with physical disabilities the opportunity to develop motor and aural skills on a real instrument. Instructionally, educators should be sure to include lessons that require minimal physical strength; this inclusive teaching strategy will encourage confidence and self-esteem for students with physical disabilities. Educational goals should be appropriately sequenced to facilitate outcomes that are realistic and achievable.

Since the student with visual impairment will not have the visual aspect to aid their learning, music educators should focus on other modalities of learning, i.e., aural and tactile methods, to help the visually impaired student succeed. If the student with visual impairment is learning how to play an instrument, the educator should allow ample time for the student to physically explore the instrument and take it apart if possible. The student should also have the chance to explore other examples of the instrument so the student can fully conceptualize the shape and various aspects of the instrument. Also, the music instructor should use the Braille Music Code for lessons on staff notation; students should not be expected to rely solely on their aural awareness of music, but should be able to learn musical notation as well. When demonstrating instrumental technique and movement, the educator should demonstrate the action by placing his or her hand under the student's hand.

Helping students with dyslexia understand written musical notation

Students with dyslexia tend to have difficulty with visual tracking, visual stress, visual-motor comprehension, sound discrimination, and symbol-sound relationships. Without the proper guidance from the music educators, the student with dyslexia may feel alienated from the educational curriculum, as well as from peers and the overall learning process. The music educator should begin by removing any barriers to the student's learning and helping to build on the student's strengths. Musical notation can be enlarged so that visual processing for the student will be easier. The student can also use color-coded overlays to prevent visual stress from an all-white background as well as to highlight certain aspects of the score. The music educator should also use a multi-sensory approach to teaching musical notation, including Dalcroze and Kodály techniques, visual and aural demonstrations of rhythm, visual and tactile demonstrations of notation, technology, pattern learning, and graphics within the notation.

Musical imitation

Improvisation cannot exist without imitation. As the very basis of improvisation, imitation allows students to learn techniques, progressions, melodic contour, and rhythmic patterns of improvisers of the past. Once the student has immersed himself or herself in studying improvisation through imitation, he or she will be much better able to assimilate improvisation techniques for innovative and new musical ideas. Students begin to learn how to imitate from birth. Language acquisition, gestures, and expressions are all learned through imitation. Therefore, as an educator, the process of teaching imitation should focus on musical selection to imitate, allowing the students to explore phrases in various keys and moods. The musical selections should give the students total immersion so that the learned framework becomes a launching point for free exploration in the next step towards full improvisation.

Musical variation

Much of improvisation consists of variation: thematic variation, melodic variation, rhythmic variation, stylistic variation, and harmonic variation are all examples of improvisational techniques. When teaching musical variation to students, the instructor should begin with only slight variations within a controlled framework. The students may start exploring variation through melodic variation first; all other aspects of the music should remain constant so the student has a foundation from which to diverge. Melodies may introduce appoggiaturas, silence, and added neighbor notes, until the melody is so varied that the only recognizable aspects are the constant harmonies. Music educators can also use the call-and-response technique for group improvisation, with each call and each response of the students a continued variation of the riff. Educators should incorporate improvisations by students in every concert or project as an extra motivator as students learn how to improvise through techniques such as variation.

Baroque improvisation vs. jazz improvisation

Baroque improvisation and jazz improvisation are separated by more than two centuries of musical development, and share widely different origins. Baroque improvisation served a primarily religious element in the churches of the time, while jazz improvisation was born in the bars and alleyways of New Orleans. Instruments used in Baroque improvisation centered on string instruments, while in jazz improvisation, a wide array of instruments can be found, from brass instruments and voices to drum kits and banjos. However, Baroque and jazz improvisation share many similar traits; although the instrumentations differ, both styles feature a more prominent section as well as a supporting harmonic section. Also, both Baroque and jazz improvisation follow a standard form in performance, whether a 32-bar form in jazz or a ritornello form in Baroque music. Throughout both genres, improvisations are based on outlined chord symbols that direct the melody.

Musical units leading to basic composition

When teaching basic composition, the curriculum should entail several introductory concepts that sequentially lead to the understanding and creation of musical patterns. The beginning lessons should cover elements of notation as well as the understanding and appreciation of musical patterns. The students should learn treble clef, meter, bar line, measure, staff, octave, and intervals. Students should also examine a theme and variation, to learn how musical patterns can function. Students should start with short eight-measure phrases, working on the sequencing and patterning of music. The instructor should use highly imaginative examples to demonstrate sound patterning, such as a percussive interpretation of a thunderstorm or the sound a hopping frog might make. As the students learn to integrate their imagination with musical sounds, the lesson sequencing can focus more on musical compositional techniques such as transcriptions, cadences, and different tonalities.

Simple and compound musical form

Simple musical form describes a tonal work that can be seen as a complete and self-contained work that is not divisible into other, smaller self-contained works. Examples of simple musical forms include binary and ternary forms. In each of these forms, there are thematic sections labeled A or B, but neither of these thematic sections can be further divisible into other simple forms. Compound musical form describes a tonal work that can be seen as a composite form that is made up of other, smaller simple forms such as binary and ternary forms. An example of a compound form is the Minuetto and Trio, in which the simple Minuetto form surrounds the simple binary Trio form to create an overall ternary compound form. Other examples of compound musical forms are sonata movements, symphony movements, string quartets, and suites.

Harmonic progression with proper root motion

There are several musical skills necessary for a student to understand in composing a harmonic progression with proper root motion. Students should understand the circle of 5ths relationship between all 24 diatonic major and minor keys. This systematic organization of keys will help the student in creating key signatures and key relationships within chord progressions. Students should also understand that scales have formulae and spellings, and whole and half tones, as well as understand the concept of diatonic harmony. Without these precursory concepts, the student will have a harder time grasping the basic diatonic harmony of a major scale with Roman numeral designations. Students should also understand all inversions of triads and seventh chords, as the composition of proper root motion assumes the incorporation of appropriate inverted chords. Also important in the composition of harmonic progressions is proper voice leading of all four SATB voices, which in turn informs the proper motion of the chord roots.

Impressionism

Impressionism began as a visual arts movement at the end of the nineteenth century and beginning of the twentieth century with the works of Edouard Manet, Claude Monte, Edgar Degas, Pierre-Auguste Renoir, Berthe Morisot, Camille Pissarro, Alfred Sisley, and Mary Cassatt. The painters of the Impressionist movement sought to move away from the highly defined traditional paintings of the official salons of the day, and to create works that caught the brief, sensory effect of a particular moment through optical effects of light, color, and atmosphere. The painters used soft brushstrokes, abandoning any sharp lines to evoke a sense of haze and smoke in their work. The Impressionist movement in the visual arts paralleled the musical movement of the nineteenth and twentieth centuries as well. In the music of Claude Debussy, formal elements such as distinct tonalities, cadences, and line were abandoned, while soft effects such as non-climactic melodies, complex textures, misty instrumental colors, and continuously changing forms all contributed to fleeting moments of color.

Ballade

The ballade refers to a literary and musical form in which words are set to three stanzas with seven or eight lines each. The original literary form of the ballade usually featured a narrative that could be comic, romantic, tragic, or historical. Although ballades have been around since the Medieval ages, renewed interest in the Romantic era helped the genre to flourish in the eighteenth and nineteenth centuries. Poets who often wrote ballades that were then set to music include Goethe, Schiller, Fontane, Heine, Platen, and Chamisso. Notable ballade composers who set literary ballades to music include Schubert, Schumann, Liszt, Wagner, and Strauss. By the middle of the nineteenth century, composers started to write purely instrumental ballades; Chopin wrote four piano ballades, most likely based on poems by Mickiewicz, and both Liszt and Brahms wrote instrumental piano ballades.

Integrating music with common core subjects

Music educators have the unique opportunity of integrating subjects outside of the fine arts with musical instruction. While focusing on musical instruction, the students can be fully immersed in musical learning as well as language arts, history, math, and science. When discussing musical phrasing, music educators can relate questions and answers in music to questions and answers in English. The students can also examine how individual phrases within music reinforce the work as a whole, the same way an individual sentence or paragraph relates to a written text as a whole. Teachers can use repertoire selections to reinforce historical knowledge as well, whether it be the Industrial Revolution during the Romantic era, or the Greek and Roman renewal of the Renaissance era. Basic musical elements require a mathematical understanding such as the division of meters and the relationship of subdivided beats. Concepts in science such as humidity, fluid dynamics, and physics can be integrated with instrument knowledge such as woodwind care and sound wave properties.

Content standards

The National Standards for Arts Education covers nine general content standards for grades K-4. Students in this age bracket should be able to sing independently and in a group on pitch and rhythm, with dynamics, articulation, and phrasing. Students should be able to perform instruments in groups with easy rhythmic, melodic, and choral patterns, while maintaining a steady tempo. Students should be able to improvise simple musical answers and accompaniment for familiar melodies. Students should be able to compose simple short songs to accompany readings or dramatizations. Students should be able to read basic notation to eighth notes, basic dynamic markings, and understand 2/4 and 4/4 meters. Students should be able to move purposefully to music and be able to identify a variety of instrumental sounds. Students should be able to explain their personal preferences to certain music with proper music terminology. Students should be able to identify similarities and differences in the various arts and other disciplines. Students should be able to identify various genres or roles of music in their daily life.

The National Standards for Arts Education covers nine general content standards for grades 5-8. Students in this age bracket should be able to sing independently and in a group accurately in two or three parts, with expression in a variety of genres. Students should be able to perform instruments independently and in groups with accuracy, expression, and good technique. Students should be able to improvise short melodies and simple harmonic accompaniments in a consistent style, meter, and tonality. Students should be able to read standard notation including sixteenth and dotted notes, and understand compound meters. Students should be able to describe and analyze specific elements of music in listening. Students should be able to evaluate their own and other students' performances based on their own criteria. Students should be able to compare and contrast music with other fine arts and other disciplines. Students should be able to classify and describe various genres and styles of music in history and other world cultures.

The National Standards for Arts Education covers nine general content standards for grades 9-12. Students in this age bracket should be able to sing a large and varied vocal repertoire in four or more parts with expression, technical accuracy, and good ensemble skills. Students should be able to perform a large and varied instrumental repertoire with technical accuracy, expression, and good ensemble skills. Students should be able to improvise original melodies and stylistically appropriate harmonizing parts in a consistent style, meter, and tonality. Students should be able to compose for a variety of instruments and voices. Students should be able to read standard and nonstandard notation in full vocal and instrumental scores. Students should be able to describe and analyze in detail specific elements of music in listening. Students should be able to critically evaluate performances, improvisations, and compositions. Students should be able to meticulously compare and contrast music with other fine arts and other disciplines. Students should be able to identify and describe various genres and styles of music in history and other world cultures through aural examples.

Cultural diversity

As the United States becomes increasingly multicultural and diverse, the role of music education should adjust its aim to encompass music and cultures from around the world. Music education in the United States has been historically focused on music of the Western world, such as that of Western classical music, American band music, and Western folk traditions. As more and more students in the American classroom come from diverse backgrounds, music educators should incorporate world music within its curriculum. Elementary music teachers can use Latin, South African, Indian, Chinese, Japanese music, etc., to illustrate basic arts standards such as singing in groups and learning musical elements. Band, choral, and orchestra directors should include non-Western musical repertoire in concerts, such as those of non-Western composers and arrangers. As the ethnic makeup of the student population diversifies, so should

- 31 -

music education diversify to reflect the multicultural aspect of modern society and not the monoculture of the distant past.

Non-formal teaching and informal learning

In contrast to a formal learning setting in which a music educator introduces educational content to a student, informal training refers to a student's self-led exploration of musical learning with or without an experienced mentor. Non-formal teaching and informal learning can constitute a valuable part of the student's growth as a musician. When students are in charge of their own musical development, they are able to choose the style and direction of their growth. This casual form of learning gives students more autonomy in their education, which encourages them to become more involved in their own learning. Many famous musicians were self-taught, and students can learn what works best for them as individuals, instead of a teacher-dictated method or form. However, educators should be careful about the potential pitfalls of disregarding formal education entirely for non-formal teaching. Since a student is entirely accountable for his or her own musical development, educational outcomes can be highly variable depending on the student. Also, students who learn informally tend to practice only those skills that are their strengths, while their weaker skills go neglected.

Adaptive technology for helping students with disabilities

The modern music classroom has paved the way for inclusive learning for students with disabilities. The use of adaptive or assistive technology allows students with disabilities and students with injuries the opportunity for music education and achievement. Many iPad applications act as a touch-sensitive synthesizer to convert movement to audio, allowing students with limited mobility or digits to create music. If a visually impaired student must move between instruments, the use of a simple string to guide the student can greatly widen the possibilities for performance. Also, sheet music can be enlarged for students with low vision, or even translated to Braille for students who are blind. For students who have trouble holding an instrument or reaching all the keys, music educators can use adaptive toggles, joysticks, clamps, and other tools to allow the student to be able to play. Hearing-impaired students can use cochlear implants, hearing aids, or vibration-based technologies to play in an ensemble.

Dalcroze method

The Dalcroze method was developed around 1900 by Swiss composer, musician, and pedagogue Émile Jaques-Dalcroze, who developed a system of music education through movement called eurhythmics, in which students use a kinesthetic approach to experience musical concepts. In the Dalcroze method, the body is seen as the instrument, and students discover expression, musicality, tempo, dynamics, style, and phrase structure through physical dialogue with the music. Without the ability to physically respond to music, Dalcroze believed that no human could be fully musical. The approach uses eurhythmics, solfege, and improvisation to facilitate musical development in children. In a typical eurhythmics class, students will incorporate movement of their feet, arms, and bodies to music that is either improvised by the teacher or played from a recording. This method was brought to the United States in the early 1900s and slowly found its way into mainstream primary-level music education.

Kodály method

The Kodály method was developed by Hungarian composer, musician, ethnomusicologist, and educator Zoltan Kodály (1882-1967), who believed that music is an innate part of every human's experience and that musical literacy should be an integral part of every child's education. For Kodály, the main goal of musical education is singing; since music belongs to every human, and every culture has folk songs, the voice is then the most accessible instrument. To facilitate musical literacy for the masses, Zoltan Kodály advocated the use of the movable-do system, hand signs for solfege syllables, rhythmic syllables, and solfa notation. The use of hand signs provides both a visual and kinesthetic tool for children so that the musical elements of pitch and intervals are first experienced and then identified. The Kodály method uses a five-step instructional sequence: Preparation, Make Conscious, Reinforcement, Practice, and Create, and is foundational in early music education philosophies today.

Orff-Schulwerk method

The Orff-Schulwerk method was developed by German composer, musician, and educator Carl Orff (1895-1982) and his close collaborator Gunild Keetman (1904-1990), who believed that music should be actively experienced and is best learned through a child's natural tendency to play. In the Orff approach, students explore music through the integration of drama, speech, and movement. Students are encouraged to play an active part in their musical development through improvisation on pitched and unpitched musical instruments. The Orff-Schulwerk method emphasizes rhythm development through chanting and bodily rhythm patterns and movement, and melodic development through improvisation of speaking patterns and specialized Orff instruments. The pentatonic scale is the most common scale used in the method, as it is most accessible on the Orff instruments. The Orff-Schulwerk approach is common in today's elementary music classrooms and is found in schools around the world.

Suzuki method

The Suzuki method was developed by Japanese violinist, educator, and composer Shinichi Suzuki (1898-1998), who believed that musical development is best structured through a mother tongue approach, where children hear and learn to play music from an early age, as with speech. The Suzuki method emphasizes substantial parent involvement, an early start, listening, and repetition, similar to a child's language development. Creating an encouraging environment immensely helps a child's musical development. Students typically begin learning music by ear, and after developing competence on an instrument, learn to read music notation. The Suzuki learning sequence follows the language learning sequence, since children learn how to speak before they learn how to read. The Suzuki method offers a sequential repertoire for musical development on a variety of instruments and is found in many schools through use of the Suzuki repertoire, memorization of pieces, repetition, learning by rote, and continual parental involvement.

Bloom's taxonomy

Bloom's taxonomy refers to the framework for educational goals and objectives for learning as set in the 1950s by Benjamin Bloom (1913-1999) and other educational psychologists. The model outlines hierarchical levels of thinking in three different domains: cognitive, affective, and psychomotor. Objectives for the cognitive domain focus on knowledge; for the affective domain, objectives focus on values; and for the psychomotor, objectives focus on physical motor skills. The model for the cognitive domain is most commonly referred to in music education as an assessment tool in forming and evaluating educational goals. The hierarchal levels in order are knowledge, comprehension, application, analysis, synthesis, and evaluation. In the knowledge stage, students must remember or recall information. In the comprehension stage, students must understand and be able to explain ideas and concepts. In the application stage, students apply the information in a new way. In the analysis stage, students must distinguish between different parts of the concept. In the synthesis stage, students must be able to gather the knowledge acquired to support and justify a decision. In the evaluation stage, students become independent to create and improvise original ideas.

David Elliot

David Elliot is a music educator and philosopher whose book, *Music Matters: A New Philosophy of Music Education*, presents the praxial philosophy of music education, a direct departure from Reimer's aesthetic philosophy of music education. Elliot endorses a practical, procedural approach to music education, one that puts emphasis on the activity of, rather than the feeling that comes from, music making. To Elliot, musical knowledge is not just about familiarity and appreciation of musical works, but is also about the direct, purposeful skill set involved in making music. Central to Elliot's praxial philosophy is the concept of musicianship – one that encompasses music making and music listening. Curriculum should be based on music practice and should start with music making before students can fully comprehend the art of music making when listening to music. Elliot recommends a student apprenticeship model of education where the teacher plays the role of mentor and expert musician.

Rudolf von Laban

Rudolf von Laban (1879-1958) was a Hungarian dancer and theorist whose foundational movement theories for dance have been adopted by music educators for movement-based music education. Laban believed that all people should learn the four elements of movement to develop mindfulness and creativity. These four elements, or "effort" elements, are flow, weight, time, and space. Flow refers to free and tense movements; weight refers to heavy and light movements; time refers to quick and slow movements; and space refers to direct/straight and indirect/arcing movement. Laban also outlined eight basic actions: punch, slash, dab, flick, press, wring, glide, and float. Although these movement theories were originally intended for dance education, music educators have used these ideas to develop curriculum that incorporates effort elements and actions to express and interpret music, as well as in performance. These movements have also been adopted by conductors to convey musical gesture.

Bennett Reimer

Bennett Reimer was a prominent music educator and philosopher whose influential book, *A Philosophy of Music Education*, promoted an aesthetic model of music education. For Reimer, music exists as an expressive form, and cannot be limited to intellectual or other non-musical pursuits. Its merit is in connecting people to feelings, and Reimer believed that because music is essentially dynamic sound waves, it is the only art form that can kindle mental feelings. Reimer argued for the integration of music in general education for the overall betterment of society's compassion and empathy. The best form of music education involves listening, examining, and actively participating in only musical works, which to Reimer ought to be expressive. In a music curriculum, performance should not be the focus, since performance itself does not encourage active listening and the development of aesthetic feeling.

Phyllis Weikart

Phyllis Weikart has written numerous books on the pedagogical applications of music and movement and is the author of *Movement Plus Music*, a music education guide for learning through movement for ages 3-7, *Round the Circle: Key Experiences in Movement*, and *Teaching Movement and Dance: A Sequential Approach to Rhythmic Movement*, among others. She has served on the faculty of the Division of Kinesiology at the University of Michigan and is also the founder of the program Education Through Movement: Building the Foundation, a research-based approach to learning through movement and music. In the Weikart method, kinesthetic experiences are broken down into individual units. First, the movements must be isolated and modeled to the students, then the movement may be simplified and built upon, and finally, the students must have a variety of opportunities to use the movements in personal and creative ways. Through her program, Weikart provides a detailed, sequential approach to movement-based musical tasks, and continues the traditions developed by Dalcroze and Orff-Schulwerk.

Utilitarian approach

The utilitarian philosophy for the inclusion of music in general educational curriculum stems from the writings of Plato and Aristotle in ancient Greece. Good character, civic responsibility, cultural awareness, and a quality of nobility were only some of the non-musical benefits of music study. For music educators who embrace a utilitarian philosophy of music education, music is a tool to develop extra-musical benefits, whether for other intellectual fields, for the development of character, or for social entertainment. Arguments in favor of this utilitarian philosophy point to the persistence, control, and aural awareness students need in order to develop musical performance skills. Students develop fine motor skills when executing instrumental performance. Comprehension skills are reinforced when students master various levels of musical complexity. Singing helps students develop deep breathing and a strong diaphragm. For supporters of a utilitarian rationale, music is a key component of a comprehensive education.

Aesthetic approach

The aesthetic philosophy for the inclusion of music in the general curriculum emerged during the national education reform of the 1950s. As schools sought to redefine general education in the U.S., music educators saw the need for a new philosophy of music education beyond what the utilitarian philosophy could provide. Influential theorists of aesthetic arts education include Bennett Reimer, Michael Mark, Elliot Eisner, Charles Leonhard, Robert House, and Maxine Greene. These scholars argued that music ought to be studied in and for itself; only through music and the arts can students develop the sensitivity, feeling, and symbolic communication represented by musical understanding. Any extra-musical benefits pale in comparison to the pure enjoyment and interaction of making music. To supporters of the aesthetic philosophy for the inclusion of music education, no other field of study can develop the musical perception, mental sensations, and the appreciation for beautiful sound except music study itself.

Fixed-do system vs. the movable-do system

In the fixed-do system of notational reading, the solmization of pitches refers to a specific pitch, usually where do refers to the C pitch, re refers to the D pitch, mi refers to the E pitch, and so on. In the movable-do system of notational reading, the solmization of pitches refers to any pitch within a diatonic scale so that do refers to the tonic, re refers to the supertonic, mi refers to the mediant, and so on. In the movable-do system, any pitch can be do, while the rest of the diatonic scale is built upon the relative tonic pitch. The fixed-do system of notational reading focuses on the functional association of the specific pitches to the staff, where do is always recognized as C. The movable-do system of notational reading focuses on the intervallic relationship between the pitches as they occur within the scale.

Incorporating solfege into regular rehearsals

When teaching an ensemble how to sight-read, it is useful to incorporate solfege into rehearsals to teach the relative relationship between pitches as they occur within any diatonic scale. The reinforcement of solfege on a movable-do system trains the student's understanding of relative pitch. As the students learn to sight-read through solfege, they will be able to identify the relative position of the pitch within a scale, without the additional processing of identifying the absolute pitch. Music educators should begin by teaching students all the solfege syllables, with the added hand motions that reinforce the spatial relationships between pitches. The solfege syllables should be reinforced by singing through a number of different keys to train the student's ears to hear the relationships between the diatonic pitches. As the lessons progress, students should be required to sing or play back certain pitch intervals in various keys, such as a do-mi-sol progression.

Instructional activities that aid intervallic reading and understanding

Intervallic reading is founded on the principle that students who can recognize the relative relationships between pitches will be able to read more quickly and with less mental processing demands than reading note by note. Students who read music note by note must first mentally identify the pitch name, translate that into the fingering or key pattern on the instrument, and then play. Students who read intervallically can forgo the pitch identification step of mental processing and proceed immediately to spatial processing, thus simplifying the reading process. Music educators can use instructional activities that reinforce the concept of spatial distance and direction, such as dictating a tune by note distance and direction only, i.e., 2nd up, 3rd down, making a game out of flash cards, being able to play intervals and directions with eyes closed, and practicing placing notes on a classroom staff.

Neural bases for mental practice efficacy

Mental practice has been shown to be a highly effective method of instrumental practicing when access to an instrument is not possible. When musicians practice traditionally on an instrument, the maxim "practice makes perfect" describes the correct pattern-forming process of the brain. Many music educators ascribe instead to the phrase "practice makes permanent," as scientists now know that repeated practicing reinforces the cognitive neural pathway of a particular action, similarly to the way habits are formed. It is therefore important for a musician to make sure to practice passages correctly, or else incorrect technique can easily be habituated by repeated practicing. The concept for mental practicing mirrors the neural processes of physical practice, and helps to reinforce a particular neural pathway even without movement. Mental practice combined with physical practice provides optimal cognitive and motor learning for a musician.

Comprehensive Musicianship through Performance

The Comprehensive Musicianship through Performance initiative is a model that prioritizes an inclusive, deeper understanding of music for lifelong musical involvement, rather than a narrow-minded exclusive learning model. In the model, the rehearsal becomes a learning laboratory with the teacher acting as a musical facilitator rather than merely as a lecturer or conductor. The chosen musical selection becomes a vessel for musical discovery; as students prepare the selection, the instructor provides a holistic approach for different objectives and different learning styles. The model encompasses a wide possibility of student outcomes, from knowledge of music history, style, and composition, to form, structure, and theory. The five main elements of the CMP educational process are music selection, objectives, analysis, strategies, and assessment. These segments may be used in any order to plan a music curriculum. Analysis involves a deeper understanding of the history, form, and style of a musical selection; the educator then decides on the learning objectives through a musical selection; strategies for musical discovery and performance are implemented in the curriculum; and the educator assesses students' needs and educational outcomes.

Gordon's Music Learning Theory

Edwin Gordon developed the Music Learning Theory to describe how students learn music and how it should be taught. The theory centers on the concept of audiation, a term Gordon uses to describe the internalization of music when performing, listening, or composing. Gordon differentiates audiation from aural perception, as aural perception is an involuntary response to sound in the brain, whereas audiation

- 36 -

requires cognitive processing in the brain to give meaning to the sound. Gordon delineates eight different types of audiation. Type 1 involves listening to familiar or unfamiliar music; Type 2 involves reading familiar or unfamiliar music; Type 3 encompasses writing familiar or unfamiliar music via dictation; Type 4 involves recalling and performing familiar music from memory; Type 5 deals with recalling and writing familiar music from memory; Type 6 involves creating and improvising unfamiliar music; Type 7 involves creating and improvising unfamiliar music while reading; and Type 8 deals with creating and improvising unfamiliar music while writing.

Orff-Schulwerk lesson plan

The Orff-Schulwerk approach to music education emphasizes children's natural tendency to play as a key component to musical discovery and development. Students are given the opportunity to explore various rhythms, melodies, and songs, and then imitate, improvise, and create their own rhythms, melodies, and songs. Central activity components of an Orff-Schulwerk lesson include speech, singing, movement, and playing instruments. The Orff approach holds that musical development begins with a child's natural speech; children use common chants and rhymes to explore rhythmic stress patterns. Along with speech, the Orff method uses singing to introduce tonal patterns and strengthen children's singing abilities. Singing activities are most commonly formatted as games and simple songs to encourage students' natural tendency to play. Movement through games is also an important activity component, as music and movement are fundamentally intertwined in the Orff-Schulwerk philosophy. The model Orff-Schulwerk activity is the use of instruments; common instruments include body percussion, hand instruments, and specialized Orff instruments built specifically to facilitate easy access for children. These include the bass, alto, and soprano xylophones and metallophones, and the soprano and alto glockenspiel.

Dalcroze eurhythmics

The Dalcroze approach to music education makes use of physical movement as a tool for musical development. Emile Jacques-Dalcroze believed that music should be taught with kinesthetic movement so that sound can be integrated with nerves and muscles, and articulated through bodily motion. Dalcroze theorized that music can be more readily understood through movement than reason, and musical education should start with movement before intellectual concepts can be introduced. In this framework, the body is the instrument, and students discover expression, musicality, tempo, dynamics, style, and phrase structure through inner dialogue with the music. In this way, students develop musicality with a deeper understanding of their physical connection to music and refine their senses of rhythm, coordination, hearing, and creativity.

Pre-K eurhythmics class

Sample activities for a Pre-K eurhythmics class can include:
- Students dance freely to a teacher's improvisation on the piano that changes frequently in relation to mood, tempo, dynamics, and style. Students must change their dance styles accordingly.
- Students must pass a beach ball around in a circle in rhythm, as defined by the teacher's music.
- Students stomp their feet in rhythm and sway side to side while the teacher recites a children's rhyme.
- Students clap their hands to the tempo of the teacher's improvisation at the piano; the teacher alters the tempo of the music so that students must follow along.

The teacher plays a soft melody on the piano while the students move smoothly to the music; for every sudden sfz chord played, students must clap hands with a partner, then resume the quiet music/movement.

Instructional and Assessment Procedures

Choral balance and choral blend

When executing good choral blend, singers must pay attention to their use of vowel modification, dynamics, and vocal vibrato. In a choral setting, pure vowel sounds are preferred in producing the sounds a, e, i, o, and u. The mouth cavity must be open with a raised palette to produce the pure vowel sounds. Additionally, dynamics among the singers must be adjusted to compensate for the stronger singers as well as the weaker singers. When singing in a choral setting, self-monitoring is key in knowing when to adjust sound levels in accordance with the surrounding musicians. Generally, vocal vibrato should be kept to a minimum when striving for good choral blend; an active vocal vibrato can easily stick out in a choral texture, and works conversely in achieving good choral blend, which should prioritize uniform sound, texture, and tone.

In a choral setting, both choral balance and choral blend are essential elements of a successful and aurally satisfactory choral performance. Both choral balance and choral blend refer to the collective sound provided from the group of singers. For a chorus to be balanced, there should be an equal level of sound coming from all ranges of voices. If a chorus is not balanced, the term "top-heavy" is used to indicate a sound that has an overabundance of soprano or alto sound, whereas the term "bottom-heavy" is used to indicate a sound that has an overabundance of tenor or bass sound. Choral blend refers to the uniformity of vowel formation and tone among the singers. Like choral balance, good choral blend is produced by the collective group; however, uniform choral blend is achieved not by the intensity of each vocal range, but by each individual singer's diligence to the same standard of tone production and blend within the entire chorus.

Singer who cannot hear himself or herself

Spacing within any chorus is of key importance in a healthy choral collaboration. If a singer cannot hear himself or herself, productive collaboration could be hindered and inaccurate intonation could become detrimental not only to the individual singer, but also to the group as a whole. If a singer cannot hear himself or herself in a choral setting, then the likelihood of actively listening and constant adjusting to the surrounding musicians becomes minimal; self-monitoring is key in productive collaboration. Also, when self-monitoring becomes hindered, then intonation can easily become a problem for the singer. If one singer becomes out of tune in a choral setting, then that voice could easily influence the surrounding singers' intonation, resulting in an entire chorus that becomes out of tune.

Instrumentalist who cannot hear himself or herself

Self-monitoring within any ensemble is of key importance in a healthy musical collaboration. If an instrumentalist cannot hear himself or herself, productive collaboration could be hindered and inaccurate tuning, rhythm, and phrasing could become detrimental not only to the individual instrumentalist, but also to the ensemble as a whole. If an instrumentalist cannot hear himself or herself in an ensemble, then the likelihood of actively listening and constant adjusting to the surrounding musicians becomes minimal; self-monitoring is key in productive collaboration. Also, when self-monitoring becomes hindered, then inaccurate tuning, rhythm, and phrasing can easily become a problem for the instrumentalist. If one instrumentalist in an ensemble becomes out of tune with inaccurate rhythm and phrasing, then that part could easily influence the surrounding musicians' tuning, rhythm, and phrasing, resulting in an entire ensemble that becomes out of tune with misaligned rhythm and phrasing.

Unified ensemble performance

For a musical ensemble performance to be unified, key musical elements such as tuning, balance, phrasing, articulation, and cut-offs must be unified. In any ensemble, tuning must be well matched, or else the sound of an out-of-tune ensemble member will noticeably intrude. The sound intensity of all the parts must be balanced for a clear melody and support accompaniment to be effective. For example, if the middle ranges of an ensemble are too loud, then the melody of the musical piece will be obscured. Phrasing is another important musical element, and if each musician is not phrasing melodies in the same manner, then there is no cohesion in the musical performance. Articulation must also be handled in the same way. If some ensemble members play a legato while others play staccato, then the texture of the musical piece becomes muddled. In the same way, if the musicians of an ensemble do not have a simultaneous onset or cutoff of the sound, then the disunity of sound becomes jarringly evident.

Conducting

As the leader of a group of musicians, the conductor plays an essential role in making music through performance or rehearsals. Several key elements of conducting technique play a vital role in coordinating various musical elements into one collective effort. At the most basic level, the conductor indicates the tempo and the meter; the conductor must have a clear beat pattern that indicates not only a steady tempo, but also the meter of the music. The conductor must also indicate preparatory beats for certain sectional or instrumental entrances as well as releases at the end of a section or phrase. Conductors must also indicate fermatas, changes in tempo, and dynamics. The conductor must also actively listen to the balance between sections and present the right cues to maintain dynamics and the proper balance. Other essential elements of conducting technique include style-specific musical interpretation, the role of the free hand, and score study.

When conducting, the position of the baton should be a natural extension of the hand and arm. It should not be rigidly in line, but should serve as a musical tool of expression; in a gentle passage, the baton may be lightly held with only the first few fingers, but in an animated passage, the baton may be tightly grasped to evoke a feeling of passion and urgency. The elbow should be slightly raised away from the body so that the baton can be clearly seen from all angles. The free hand without the baton plays the role of musical reinforcement and can also help turn pages. As an independent stimulus, the free hand can reinforce dynamics such as crescendos and decrescendos, as well as aid in cueing parts. The free hand should also indicate releases, phrasing, musical style, and necessary modifications in the balance of the ensemble.

When conducting an ensemble, careful attention should be made to bodily posture so that no slight imbalance or awkward position will detract from the clear musical cues from the conductor. The conductor's feet should be about shoulder width with one foot slightly more forward to maintain optimal balance. The knees should not bend, and equal weight should be given to each foot. The conductor's spine should be tall and erect. Just before beginning, the arms should be in an attention position using both the baton hand and the free hand held ready to indicate the preparatory beat. The arms should not be too close to the body and should be held up and out at a comfortable width. The elbows should be slightly forward ready to engage the ensemble. The wrists should be flexible and neither limp nor stiff.

It is of utmost importance to provide a clear attack while conducting an ensemble. Without a precise indication of the ictus, the ensemble will not begin to play the music together and may continue to approximate the tempi and rhythms, resulting in a disorderly performance. To give a clear attack in conducting, the conductor must give a preparatory beat. During this imaginary preceding beat, the arm must move fluidly in exactly the same tempo as the intended beginning tempo; this way, the musician can easily judge the preparation movement and downbeat. The conductor should breathe in on the preparatory beat along with the ensemble and indicate the attack with equally suggestive bodily language such as direct eye contact and a head nod. The conductor must be careful to place gestural emphasis on the attack and only a slight movement on the preparatory beat.

When conducting a fermata, several considerations should be made: the tempo and presence or absence of a ritardando, the length of the fermata, the presence or absence of a rest after the fermata, and resuming tempo if the music continues. If the fermata is on the last note of the piece, the conductor should gesture in a circular motion downward as long as the fermata is to be held. If the music continues after a fermata without a break, the conductor should gesture slightly outward and upward to incorporate the preparation beat for the next note. If the music continues after a fermata with a rest, the conductor should indicate a cutoff and resume with the preparation beat in the intended tempo of the next section. Effort should be made to eliminate any awkward movements so that the musicians can comfortably play a fermata for the length indicated.

In conducting, the release of a note is as important as the initial attack; clear indication must be made on the conductor's part so that the musician does not have any doubt when to release a note. When indicating a release, the conductor should also use a preparatory beat to indicate the cutoff. A release usually comes after holding a long note; as such, the conductor's baton should indicate the final note to be played, then be held in position for as long as the note is to be held with a possible slight movement outwards. The preparatory beat to indicate the release should be a slight movement upwards so as not to detract from the musical expression of the final note. As the conductor's baton comes down or out from the preparatory beat, the stress of the cutoff marks the point of the release.

The conductor's role in directing an ensemble encompasses all musical interpretation, from tempo and balance to dynamics and expression. As such, a conductor's technique greatly influences an ensemble's performance of a musical piece. When indicating a forte or fortissimo, the conductor's gestures should be similarly bigger and "louder." The conductor can use the free hand to aid in ensemble response by signaling for more. When indicating a piano or pianissimo, the conductor's gestures should be similarly smaller and "softer." The conductor can use the free hand to aid in ensemble response by signaling for less. Body language plays an important part in eliciting dynamic and expressive contrast from the ensemble. A forte gesture can be made passionately sorrowful with heavy movements in the arms and a somber expression in the face; likewise, a forte can be made joyful and exuberant with light movements in the arms and lifted eyebrows in the face.

In conducting, there are several types of gestural indications: preparatory beats, active beats, and passive beats. Conductors use preparatory beats to ready an ensemble before an attack and before a release to allow the ensemble to anticipate the cutoff of a held note. Preparatory beats should indicate the tempo, style, and expression of the music to be played. Conductors use active beats to signal an immediate change or action from the ensemble. Typical changes that may be indicated by an active beat include marcato, legato, staccato, and accents. Passive beats are beats that do not require an immediate change from the ensemble but help to indicate things like rests, offbeats, and other simple pulses. The conscientious conductor should use all three types of beats in variation to elicit musical changes such as sectional transitions, syncopations, hemiolas, and other important musical events.

Various conducting patterns: 2/4, ¾, 4/4, 6/8, and 9/8

In a 2/4 pattern, the hand moves downward on the first beat and upward on the second beat. In a ¾ pattern, the hand moves downward on the first beat, outward on the second beat, and upward on the third beat. In a 4/4 pattern, the hand moves downward on the first beat, inward on the second beat, outward on the third beat, and upward on the fourth beat. In a compound 6/8 pattern, the hand moves downward on the first primary strong beat, bounces inward on the second and third beats, moves outward on the secondary strong fourth beat, bounces outward on the fifth beat, and upwards on the sixth beat. In a compound 9/8 pattern, the hand moves downward on the first primary strong beat, bounces inward on the second and third beats, moves outward on the secondary strong fourth beat, bounces outward on the fifth and sixth beats, then moves upward on the tertiary strong seventh beat, and bounces upward and inward on the weak eighth and ninth beats.

Conducting beat patterns

When conducting certain beat pattern, there are several principles to keep in mind. The downbeat of the pattern always indicates the strongest pulse of the pattern, and is indicated by a downward stroke of the hand. Also, the last beat of the pattern is always the weakest pulse of the pattern and is thus indicated by an upward stroke of the hand. If in a compound meter there exists a secondary strong pulse, then the movement of the hand is almost just as strong of a downbeat as the primary strong downbeat. The movement of the hand in a three- or four-beat pattern moves so that collisions between the baton hand and the free hand are avoided. Conductors may choose to indicate subdivided pulses such as eight pulses in a slow 4/4 movement, or to indicate fewer pulses in a fast movement, such as conducting only the downbeats of a fast ¾ waltz.

Determining the number of beats to conduct based on tempo

Though there are standard beat patterns in the art of conducting technique, the pattern that conductors choose to conduct should be determined by tempo, style, and meter. In a 2/4 meter, the conductor could indicate every beat; if the 2/4 meter is taken at vivace, however, it would be impractical to conduct every beat, and an indication of the downbeat would suffice. Excessive movements could convey heaviness, which could slow down the ensemble. If, however, the 2/4 meter is taken at adagio, the conductor could facilitate rhythmic fluidity and continuity by doubling the number of beats, indicating the quarter-note subdivision for a 4/4 beat pattern, so that forward movement is not lost. In general, the faster the tempo, the fewer number of beats the conductor should indicate; the slower the tempo, the higher number of beats the conductor should indicate.

Studying a score to conduct

Through score study, the conductor must analyze, reanalyze, interpret, learn, and know every detail and nuance in the music. There are several techniques that can aid the conductor in score study. During the learning process, the conductor can play all the vocal parts together on the piano to be able to listen to voice leading and harmonic changes. The conductor can also play the accompaniment part separately on the piano so that special attention can be given to the accompaniment when the entire ensemble plays. If there is text, the conductor can read the text aloud poetically so as to examine the ideal dramatic inflection and stress of the line. The conductor can analyze the score structurally, harmonically, dynamically, and melodically to know the music thoroughly. The conductor can also mark the score extensively to help mentally note all aspects of the music.

The use of other recordings as part of score study has certain advantages and disadvantages. An unfamiliar piece of music may be made more acquainted through listening to an existing performance. If the conductor is developing his or her own interpretation of the music, this may be informative in terms of tempo and style; however, this may also contribute to a "parrot" interpretation where the conductor has not made his or her own in-depth interpretation. Also, this may lead to other imitated musical characteristics that may not be historically or stylistically accurate, as every performance is framed by the conductor's interpretation. However, using recordings in score study can be an informative source of past interpretations and should not become an exact template from which to copy.

As a conductor, one of the foremost responsibilities in leading an ensemble musically is having an in-depth understanding of the music. One of the musical aspects a conductor should know scrupulously is the instrumentation and transpositions of the scored instruments. Another important musical facet to know is the form of the work; knowing the form will generate a deeper understanding of the development of the theme. Special attention should be given to analyze the harmonic and melodic structure of the work. The conductor can then easily listen to the balance of the ensemble. The conductor should also know the dynamics of the score to be able to prepare the ensemble to execute changes in sound. The conductor must also study phrase structure and any other special instrument execution.

When studying the score, there are several useful resources the conductor can use. For a thorough understanding of the historical background and performance practices, conductors can refer to scholarly books, journals, and articles to research the background of the musical work. Many musical works also have ties to extra-musical art forms such as literature, dance, visual art, and theater. Researching all sources of musical inspiration will only aid the conductor's interpretation and understanding of the score. The conductor can also use recordings of the musical work in researching performance practices and stylistic differences of past performances. If the musical work was written by a living composer, the conductor can also interview the composers themselves to delve deeper into a thorough understanding of the score. Also, conductors can consult conducting texts for a relevant perspective of the musical score.

When using recordings in score study, careful discretion must be made so that the conductor does not merely copy the interpretation of the recording. Several techniques can be applied when using recordings to prevent a "parrot" version of an existing performance. The conductor should listen to more than one interpretation of a piece to have a wide variety of interpretations. Also, the conductor should not practice conducting to the recording, as muscle memory can impede the personal development of the conductor's own interpretation. The conductor should not adhere only to famous recordings or famous conductors; effort should be made to listen to a variety of recordings. Another helpful technique is to listen early in the score study and then stop once rehearsals have begun to be able to develop one's own interpretation.

Conductor's musical interpretation

The role of conductor as musical interpreter requires adept conducting technique and a solid conviction of his or her own understanding of the music. In forming an interpretation of the music, the conductor must consider the stylistic elements of the music. Note durations, stresses, tempo, articulation, phrasing, dynamics, and other nuances all make up the necessary musical elements for a conductor to direct an ensemble well. Additionally, the conductor's own vision of the musical work should be made clear through the ensemble's performance. The conductor's own understanding of the progression of the music, its beginnings, climaxes, and endings, should all inform the execution of all musical elements. The conductor should understand the historical background of the music as well as the essence of the music itself. Interpretation takes creativity, imagination, musical flexibility, and an intimate understanding of the emotions of the music.

Score marking

In preparation for rehearsing a musical work, the conductor should mark the score for his or her own benefit; this saves time as well as processing energy when in rehearsals. During score study, the conductor should mark any or all of the following elements to prepare for the rehearsal process: entrances of sections, entrances of melodies and important themes, tutti sections, dynamic changes, fermatas, repeats, cadenzas, meter changes, tempo changes, sectional changes, harmonic structure, melodic structure, rhythmic structure, form, textual emphases, instrumentation changes, key changes, balance changes, style indications, free-hand cues, fermatas, and special preparatory beats. It may not be necessary to mark every change in the music; however, the score should be marked to the needs of each conductor to ensure a thorough analysis of the musical score.

Ostinato

An ostinato is defined as a short, repeating accompaniment pattern throughout a musical work that can consist of a simple rhythmic, melodic, or harmonic idea. Similar to a drone, the ostinato provides a stable foundation for the main melody line(s). In terms of improvisation, the ostinato is a practical tool for creating new ideas and melodies as the repeated figures stay constant, allowing the melody line to focus on a free delivery. When an ostinato is used in Baroque music, it is termed the basso ostinato, or ground bass, and can feature both harmonic and melodic properties. When an ostinato is used in jazz music, it is termed the riff or vamp, and helps to form the framework for a tune. Ostinatos are also found extensively in world music such as that of Africa and India.

Arpeggiation

An arpeggio is defined as a chord that is played note by note, successively instead of simultaneously. Also termed a broken chord, the arpeggio can be played from the highest note to the lowest note, but is more commonly played from the lowest note to the highest note. When using arpeggiation in accompaniment, the musician plays individual chords as arpeggios. If accompanying a single instrument, arpeggiation can be a practical musical technique as the arpeggio fills out the texture of the sound and adds forward motion to the music, as the chords become single notes flowing through one another instead of a simple blocked chord that must be sustained. Arpeggios also tend to soften the delivery of the accompaniment, giving the music a sense of lightness such as that of arpeggiated harp music.

Blocked chords

Blocked chords are defined as pitches that are played simultaneously like a chord. When using blocked chords in accompaniment, the player can combine notes that are written separately into a blocked chord, or play blocked chords from a chord chart. If the player must sight-read music, blocking the chords can help to simplify the sight-reading process so that the player doesn't have to read every single note; a quick scan of the harmony is all that is required to play a blocked chord of that harmony. If the player is reading music with a chord chart, then blocking chords can also provide a quick and simple method of accompaniment. The player must only see the written harmony needed, and play the blocked harmony without the intermediate processing stage of notation.

Establishing classroom rules

When teaching music in a group setting, it is always important to establish classroom rules and consequences in the beginning. The music educator should thoroughly explain expectations for the classrooms, detailing examples of good behavior and class participation. During this discussion, the music

- 43 -

educator should also explain the consequences of inappropriate behavior or negative responses to rules so that the students know the system of classroom rules from the first day. Although positive reinforcement should be emphasized in classroom management, the educator may need to use negative reinforcement in certain situations. If a student responds negatively to classroom rules, the educator may try positive reinforcement first. If this is not effective, the teacher may have to remind the entire class of the rules and consequences. If this is not effective, then the teacher may have to talk individually to the student, reinforcing the rules and taking action on the consequences of not following the rules.

Student exhibiting behavior problems

When a student misbehaves in a classroom setting, it is always important for the music educator to reflect on the misbehavior. If an adjustment in teaching style or lesson sequencing will redirect the misbehavior, then the educator should start there. The teacher should also observe for any learning impairments that may trigger behavior problems. Also, the educator should make sure to set clear limits and boundaries of behavior. If the student is misbehaving regardless of various strategies of engaging teaching techniques and sequencing, then the educator should address the misbehavior, taking care not to condemn the student but rather the behavior. The music educator should make sure not to interrupt the flow of the lesson but to address the misbehaving student with as little verbal response as possible; the teacher can use silence, physical cues, close proximity, and quickly stating the student's name as reminders to focus. If these techniques are not effective, then the teacher should thoroughly address the misbehavior after class.

Every Pupil Responds instructional technique

Educators use the Every Pupil Responds instructional technique as a way to ensure student inclusion during a lesson. The technique requires students to simultaneously respond to the teacher's question by demonstrating or displaying the appropriate response. This allows the educator to quickly and efficiently check for understanding. The Every Pupil Responds technique can be adapted to fit a variety of situations and keeps students actively involved. Teachers can hand out cards with the answers "yes" or "no," different musical notational signs, or a blank board with which students can write their own responses and hold up. Additionally, teachers can instruct students to point to the correct object or placement on an instrument. If students are seated in pairs, teachers can instruct students to whisper the answer to their neighbor, and then have the entire classroom say the answer out loud.

Procedures and routines

Classroom procedures and routines are important for structure and organization within a student's day. Daily routines and procedures can also prevent many of the misbehaviors that result from an unorganized schedule and distractions. The lessons will have less interruption from distracted students and will flow much more easily. The music teacher should make sure to establish clear procedures and routines from the first day, taking care to go over each procedure in detail while modeling the procedures to ensure full understanding from the students. The first few weeks may require more time spent establishing procedures and routines, to help the rest of the school year flow more easily. Example classroom routines that are useful in providing structure and organization include how to enter the classroom, beginning work, roll call, announcements, "tardies," absences, teacher's attention signal, leaving one's seat, assignments, supplies, group work, and independent work.

Extrinsic motivation

Extrinsic motivation is defined in behavioral psychology as motivation that exists for an individual apart from the activity or task such as an outside pressure or reward, as opposed to intrinsic motivation in which motivation exists in the activity itself. When students are extrinsically motivated, satisfaction lies in an external reward, pressure, or some external prompt. Music educators can facilitate or encourage extrinsic motivation in the classroom, especially when there is a lack of intrinsic motivation. Oftentimes, the classroom structure is based on extrinsic motivation, through rewards such as grades, privileges, and peer esteem. Extrinsic motivation can also exist through a student's sense of future well-being and goals. If the music educator focuses on extrinsic motivators such as tangible rewards or a student's ego, the motivation will disappear when the motivators disappear. Thus, educators should encourage extrinsic motivators such as the student's acknowledgement of the tasks' importance towards a future goal.

Intrinsic motivation

Intrinsic motivation is defined in behavioral psychology as motivation that exists for an individual in the activity itself, as opposed to extrinsic motivation in which motivation for an activity exists apart from the activity such as an outside pressure or reward. When students are intrinsically motivated, there will be satisfaction in the activity or task at hand, partly from a natural curiosity and partly from gratification in doing the task. Music educators can facilitate or encourage intrinsic motivation in the classroom; however, this type of motivation is only effective for those students who already have a natural tendency towards the task at hand. For other students who find no internal satisfaction or curiosity for the task at hand, intrinsic motivation will be useless. Intrinsic motivation, when effective, can foster a high quality of learning and creativity in students.

Motivating students

As a music educator, it is important to provide motivation for students in the music classroom, since motivated students result in higher engagement and better learning. One effective strategy for motivating students is to become a role model for the students; when the students see the excitement and passion for the lesson material, that energy will be transferred to the students. Another strategy is to know the students well; once the students know that the teacher is involved in their education, they will be motivated to do well. Also, the teacher should use positive reinforcement and constructive criticism. These nonjudgmental remarks should motivate students on ways to improve. The music educator should also use frequent activities where the students have the opportunity to demonstrate their achievements, encouraging them to progress to the next level in cooperation. The teacher should also set realistic performance goals, ones that are appropriately challenging but still attainable.

Semester assessment plan

Music educators should use assessment strategies that include both individual student achievement as well as group ensemble achievement. A comprehensive rubric provides accountability for each student's musical growth within an ensemble setting. A sample semester assessment plan should include individual grading criteria such as performance of technical scales and musical excerpts, correct pitch matching, and correct rhythm matching. Students should be able to demonstrate historical and contextual knowledge of the appropriate music, and should demonstrate thoughtful analysis and evaluation of music. Group grading criteria can include attendance at performances, attendance at local concerts, chamber music participation, and solo/ensemble festival participation. Classroom criteria can include rehearsal preparation and readiness. The weight of each section could be graded as follows: individual performance: 30 percent; ensemble performance: 30 percent; classroom participation: 30 percent; other: 10 percent.

Teacher feedback

Assessments in the music classroom can be a time-consuming activity; thus, it is highly useful and efficient to integrate as many informal assessment techniques as possible throughout the music rehearsal. Informal assessments can take the form of teacher feedback, short on-the-spot quizzes, and informal questioning and discussion. Not only will these informal assessments keep the students accountable for their daily musical progress, they will also give the music educator a formative assessment of the students' progress. When giving short on-the-spot performance tests, the teacher has the opportunity to gauge the progress of the individual or section; the educator can provide quick succinct feedback on accuracy, technique, or any other issues that arise. Informal questioning and discussion relating to the analysis of the music also allows the teacher to assess and provide the appropriate feedback to help the students' comprehension of the matter. The more feedback the teacher can provide, the more learning opportunities will be provided for the students.

Music performance outcomes dictating assessment components

The National Association for Music Education has published Performance Standards of musical outcomes and student abilities by grade level. These Performance Standards should provide a guideline for the music educator for assessment criteria. Students should be able to sing alone and with others, demonstrating correct technical and musical ability and in a wide range of styles. Students should be able to play an instrument alone and with others, demonstrating correct technical and musical ability and in a wide range of styles. Students should be able to improvise basic melodies and basic accompaniments on their instrument or through singing. Students should be able to compose and arrange music within specific contexts with or without technology. Students should be able to read and notate music appropriate to their level. Students should be able to listen to music and then analyze or describe it. Students should be able to evaluate music and musical performances. Students should also be able to relate music to non-musical fields such as history, visual art, literature, and others.

Successfully performing a piece of music

In order to successfully perform a piece of music, a student must know more than correct notes and rhythm. The student should also analyze all aspects of the melody, rhythm, harmony, and form of the piece. A thorough analysis of the melody, for example, can inform the performer of where the climax is, allowing the performer to appropriately time the musical tension and release of the overall piece. Knowing the rhythmic form also allows the performer to note any subtle transitions the composer may be suggesting. The harmony of the musical work also holds clues as to the structure of the work, allowing the performer to bring the appropriate mood in transitions and development of the work. The performer should also examine the historical context of the piece; knowing the intention and purpose of the composition can inform the musician as to how to execute dynamics, articulations, and releases, depending on the given mood.

Incorporating music theory instruction during a full rehearsal

As a music educator, it is important to incorporate music theory instruction during full rehearsals, ensuring that a student's musical education is a comprehensive, all-encompassing one, and not one solely focused on performance. A thorough musical education will allow the student an informed and deeper understanding of music. When possible, the music educator should introduce new theoretical concepts before rehearsing a piece; the instructor should not take too much time in explanation, but give only concise, direct introduction, as the immersion within the music will aid in a student's understanding. When the music educator interrupts the rehearsal to do spot checks, the instructor should use appropriate language in explaining the technical or musical problem, to further integrate the concept of music theory into musical performance and understanding. When time allows, the music educator can give brief verbal quizzes, to keep the students accountable for their musical theory learning.

Improvisation

Musical creativity holds improvisation at the core of its internal process through the formation of new ideas, sounds, and direction. Improvisation is the core vehicle of creativity within the musical realm. A musician might explore musical creativity by exploring only the black keys on a keyboard; this keeps the tonal context within a simple pentatonic scale and allows the musician to explore various phrases, ideas, and ranges of the keyboard. Improvisation can also foster freer musical creativity through singing or playing along to an existing track. This structured approach allows the musician to explore different timbres, harmonies, and tones with freedom. The musician must use mental imagery and mystery when improvising, to conceptualize new and different feelings, moods, and sounds. All of these processes contribute to an overall expansion of a musician's musical creativity and improvisational possibility, leading to more independent melodic, harmonic, and rhythmic improvisation.

Influence of the conductor on an ensemble

In addition to coordinating the rhythmic timing of players and other musical logistics, part of the conductor's role is to establish the emotional content and musical expression of the performance. A skilled conductor is able to extract the appropriate musical expression from the ensemble with the slightest of gestures. The conductor should utilize his or her entire body in conveying the musical expression of the piece. An energetic musical section might require the conductor to exaggerate movements in a quicker manner, with an animated expression on the face, to draw out a similar energetic mood from the players. Likewise, a somber musical section might require the conductor to conduct with heavier, slower movements, with a grave expression on the face, to draw out a similar dark and solemn sound from the players.

Socratic method

The Socratic method refers to the philosophy of education as set by the ancient Greek philosopher Socrates, which advocates the use of questions in developing a student's critical thinking and intellect. Rather than lecturing or telling the student educational content, the questions compel the student to use critical thinking for a solution or answer. The music educator can utilize this philosophy of education in all areas of music education, and especially in guided listening to teach students self-assessment, critical thinking, and how to develop one's own musical expression. Music educators can ask guided questions such as "How does the expressive elements of this performance inform your own playing?" to foster a sense of self-assessment in the student's music listening. Asking open-ended questions rather than yes/no questions will further develop the student's critical thinking abilities and intellectual curiosity, translating the analysis of guided listening to his or her own musical practice and growth.

Musical aesthetics and expression

Music educators can use various techniques to teach musical aesthetics and expression in their students. Instructors should use the technique of modeling often, to demonstrate various physical and aural attributes of an expression to the student. The student should have various visual and aural models of expressive representation to be able to integrate the technique and sound into his or her own expressive voice. The music educator can also use guided listening to teach musical aesthetics to students. As another method of modeling, the student will be able to listen to the individual expression of other performers in developing one's own musical aesthetic. The music educator can also analyze, reflect, and evaluate musical performances together with the students, so that the students will be able to think critically and creatively in analyzing, reflecting, and evaluating their own unique musical aesthetic and expression.

Long exposure over time to high dB

As a musician, it is extremely important to be aware of the risks of long exposure over time to high dB listening experiences, as high dB listening experiences occur almost daily for some musicians through band practice and rock concerts. When the inner ear is exposed to high dB sound over time, irreversible damage can occur in the nerve fibers and structures of the inner ear. Since damage that occurs over time is a gradual process, a musician may not be aware of hearing loss until it has already occurred. Symptoms include distorted or muffled hearing, difficulty hearing high-pitched sounds such as doorbells, bird chirps, and alarm clocks, pain or ringing in the ear after exposure to excessively loud sounds, and trouble understanding group conversations or conversations on the phone.

The ear and its hearing mechanisms provide a unique and essential role for the musician; deliberate measures should be taken to protect hearing and avoid permanent damage that can occur over time when exposed to high dB listening experiences. Musicians should limit band practices to two hours, as the average sound intensity of a band practice is 90 decibels, a potentially hazardous level of sound if experienced frequently over long periods of time. If musicians must practice at high sound levels frequently or for a long period of time, proper hearing protection should be used, such as earplugs and earmuffs. Musicians should also avoid listening to music on portable music devices at high volume levels, or levels above 85 decibels, for a long period of time. Damage that occurs to the inner ear cannot be medically or surgically corrected and constitutes permanent hearing loss.

Vocal health

Vocal health should be a central priority for singers and non-singers alike. As a unique organ and instrument, the voice plays an essential role in daily communication as well as in music making. An unhealthy voice can become raspy, hoarse, strained, or raw, presenting difficulty in singing and in speech. Proper hydration should be maintained to clear the mucus and moisturize the throat. Find alternatives to yelling, such as clapping, ringing a bell, or moving close to the person. Reduce background noise so that the voice does not need to be raised. Make sure to get proper rest for both the vocal mechanisms and the body through ample sleep time. Avoid drinking excessive alcohol, smoking, and inhaling chemical fumes that dehydrate and can damage the lungs. Be sure not to sing loudly on any high pitch that feels strained or uncontrolled.

Professional and Instructional Resources

Encyclopedias and dictionaries of music

Authoritative encyclopedias and dictionaries of music include the following. *The Garland Encyclopedia of World Music* is a 10-volume series of encyclopedic reference material covering all world music. Started in 1988, it is generally regarded as the authoritative source for information regarding ethnomusicology. *The New Grove Dictionary of Music and Musicians*, first published under a different name in 1879, is the authoritative reference work for Western music, with over 20 volumes. *The New Grove Dictionary* is available online through Grove Music Online and is now a part of Oxford Music Online. The Oxford Music Online is a web resource containing several reference works covering a broad range of musical topics. Online resources through Oxford Music Online include Grove Music Online, The Oxford Dictionary of Music, and The Oxford Companion to Music. *The Encyclopedia of Popular Music*, initiated in 1989 as a popular music counterpart to the definitive *New Grove*, is an authoritative reference work for all popular music, including rock, pop, jazz, hip-hop, reggae, blues, electronica, and heavy metal.

Periodical databases

Indispensable periodical databases for music history and literature include the following. JSTOR, also known as Journal Storage, is a digital database that holds 32 scholarly journals dedicated to music and includes complete back runs of the journals' contents. Titles include *Early Music History*, *Music Analysis*, *The Musical Quarterly*, *Perspectives of New Music*, and *The Journal of Musicology*, among others. The Music Index Online is a source for music periodicals and literature from 1973 to the present and contains over 655 international music journals. The International Index of Music Periodicals is another important database and indexes over 425 scholarly and popular music periodicals, including *International Journal of Music Education*, *Ethnomusicology*, *Jazz Education Journal*, *Rock and Rap Confidential*, and *Rolling Stone*. For the nineteenth and twentieth centuries, The RIPM: Retrospective Index to Music Periodicals provides a valuable resource for scholarly writing on music history and culture, holding over 200 music periodicals in its database.

Repertoire International des Sources Musicales Online

The Repertoire International des Sources Musicales Online is a musical database founded in Paris in 1952. It is one of the largest non-profit organizations of its kind and operates internationally to document musical sources from around the world. The RISM publications are divided into three series. Series A is arranged by composer and includes printed music (Series A/I) and music manuscripts (Series A/II). Series B is arranged by topic, such as ancient Greek music theory or manuscripts in lute tablature. Series C is an index of music libraries, private collections, and archives from around the world. The largest portion of the RISM inventory is Series A/II, consisting of over 380,000 manuscripts by over 18,000 composers, theorists, and librettists after 1600. The Series A/II is now an online searchable database that lists the composer or author's name, title, origin, and holding library for every entry.

RILM Abstracts of Music Literature

The RILM Abstracts of Music Literature, also known as Répertoire International de Littérature Musicale, is an international database focused on scholarship from around the world relating to any aspect of the musical discipline. This includes historical musicology, ethnomusicology, instruments and voice, music therapy, and dance. The international bibliography contains books, catalogs, master's theses, doctoral dissertations, articles, bibliographies, films, videos, ethnographic recordings, conference proceedings, reviews, Festschriften, technical drawings, facsimile editions, and iconographies. The entries are presented in the original language with an English translation of the title, an abstract, and the full bibliographic data. The online searchable database, which covers over 780,000 entries in over 117 languages from 1967 to the present, requires a subscription and is regularly updated.

Fair use provision in the 1976 Copyright Act

In the "fair use" provisions as set by the 1976 Copyright Act, educators are exempt from certain copyright laws, given the appropriate use and distribution of the copyrighted materials. When reproducing materials for use within the classroom, teachers are allowed to make copies of up to 10 percent of the entire work for each student, but cannot reproduce an entire copyrighted work for the classroom. When recording copyrighted materials, educators are exempt from the compulsory license only if the educator makes a single recording. If the educator wants to make more than one copy but fewer than 500, the educator should contact the publisher. To make more than 500 copies of the recording, the educator must obtain a license from the Harry Fox Agency. The educator is allowed to rearrange a musical work in a reasonable way for educational purposes. The educator is allowed to perform a copyrighted song only if for demonstration in the classroom; all other performances require a license.

Licensing resources

NMPA stands for the National Music Publishers' Association, which represents many of the music publishers in the United States and helps with copyright holder identification. The MPA, the Music Publishers' Association of the United States, similarly represents many print music publishers in the nation and also assists in copyright ownership issues. The ASCAP (American Society of Composers, Authors, and Publishers), the BMI (Broadcast Music, Inc.), and the SESAC (Society of European Stage Authors and Composers) all function to exercise appropriate performance licensing and distribution to their publishers and members. The HFA, the Harry Fox Agency, primarily serves as a recording license resource for many of the U.S. music publishers. The U.S. Copyright Office is a part of the Library of Congress and provides general information on copyright laws and issues in the United States.

Maintaining student confidentiality and appropriate professional conduct

Music educators are entrusted to oversee the growth, development, and well-being of the students, and as such, have certain moral and ethical obligations. The music educator should act in the highest professional manner with a commitment to the music education profession, to the students, to the community, and to the family. Since music educators can be seen as role models to developing a student's musical growth, all boundaries between student and teacher should be honored so that both parties can be held above reproach. The music educator should act in a way to ensure an emotionally and physically safe and healthy environment for the students. When travelling to field trips and concerts, the students must ride in a district-approved vehicle and never in a personal vehicle. When greeting students, the teacher should exercise minimal physical contact, again, to be above reproach.

Music educators are entrusted to oversee the development and well-being of students, and as such, have certain moral and ethical obligations to both the students as well as the community and family. The music educator should act in the highest professional manner with a commitment to the music education profession, while understanding his or her influence on the community and family. Music educators should obey all local, state, and federal laws, and should never put students in physical or emotional harm. When the music educator is in a non-school setting, he or she should continue to act with the highest level of judgment, since personal misconduct can lead to public disapproval and thus an interruption in the student's musical development and trust. Also, the music educator should never disclose a student's personal information to any person other than school personnel, for risk of a confidentiality breach. The music educator should always maintain appropriate communication with the family, and never for personal gain or advantage.

Professional organizations for music educators

The American String Teachers Association is the largest professional organization for string teachers and offers journals, books, posters, and conferences, providing ongoing training for string teachers and promoting orchestra programs in schools and communities. The Association of Teaching Artists is a professional organization for "teaching artists" in all arts disciplines – music, dance, theater, visual arts, poetry, etc. – that provides a network and place for collaboration among all its members. The Jazz Education Network is a relatively new professional organization for jazz teachers, with conferences and festivals throughout the nation. The Music Teachers National Association is a professional organization supporting music teachers across the nation, providing conferences, festivals, and programs. The National Association for Music Education has 50 state affiliates and supports music educators in schools. The American Orff-Schulwerk Association is an organization dedicated to preserving the Orff-Schulwerk approach to music education.

Attending clinics and conventions

As a music educator, it is highly beneficial to attend clinics and conventions as resources for music education. Conventions offer ample opportunities to network with fellow music educators, which result in the exchange of teaching ideas, programs, and other helpful pedagogical ideas. Networking also allows the music educator the chance to collaborate with other colleagues, opening the door for inviting guest artists to the music program. Networking also allows the music educator to find a mentor as well as to become a mentor to a new aspiring teacher. Clinics offer a multitude of benefits to both the music educator and to the participating ensemble. Clinics offer a way for ensembles to get an unbiased critique on a performance, while the music educator also gets professional feedback for an ensemble. Clinics allow both music educators and the ensemble to hear many other ensembles perform, giving both the teacher and student a peer review of the quality and level of the student's performances.

Music education journals

The Journal of Research in Music Education is a major peer-reviewed research journal in the field of music education published by Sage Publications for the National Association for Music Education. *The Music Educators Journal* is a peer-reviewed journal published by Sage as part of the National Association for Music Education, featuring scholarly and practical articles on music teaching. *The International Journal of Music Education* is another scholarly peer-reviewed journal published quarterly by Sage as part of the International Society of Music Education. *The Bulletin of the Council for Research in Music Education* is an academic journal covering peer-reviewed original research in the field of music education that is published quarterly by the University of Illinois Press for the Council for Research in Music Education. *The Journal of Band Research* features scholarly articles on band music, history, and methodology, and is the official publication of the American Bandmasters Association.

Collaborating with colleagues

Music education cannot exist in isolation. A single instructor, though dedicated and focused in delivering a high-quality curriculum, cannot meet the educational demands of all the students alone. Collaboration is advantageous in music education for various reasons. When collaborating with veteran colleagues, a music teacher can learn valuable educational strategies that only come with long-term experience. Music selection, behavior management, and instructional assessment are all areas that a willing, humble, and open collaboration can enhance. Students will also benefit when music teachers collaborate with instructors from other school subjects, whether math, English, or history. When educational objectives are reinforced within another classroom, learning is heightened, and the students learn that no one subject exists in the world in isolation – everything is interconnected. A music educator can also collaborate with the school librarian in asking for current resources, and the librarian can better understand what materials to best supply the music department. Every individual has a unique set of strengths and talents; by collaborating with colleagues, the music curriculum can become an inspired agent for student transformation.

IEPs

According to the Individuals with Disabilities Education Act, schools must provide students who have learning disabilities with the same educational opportunities as their typically developing classmates. After the initial assessment, a unique educational program is developed for each student with special needs, called the Individualized Education Program (IEP). The IEP outlines educational goals and other services or strategies needed for the student to achieve those goals. As a music educator, involvement with support staff and faculty regarding a student's IEP greatly enhances the quality of music education a student with special needs receives. The more a music educator understands a student's learning disability and techniques to aid musical learning, the more the student can engage in musical development. The music educator can collaborate with music therapists, special education teachers, and school counselors to better design special educational programs and receive consultant, direct service, and in-service assistance.

Parent-teacher conferences

Parental involvement is one of the most important factors in student success in school. When parents participate in their children's educational process, children learn from their most important support figures and gain encouragement, self-esteem, and a role model for a lifetime. One-way music teachers can influence and nurture parental support in their students' education through parent-teacher conferences. Many techniques for successful parent-teacher conferences can be used to open two-way communication in helping parents support their student's learning process. First, teachers must help parents be aware of conference dates and goals. Multiple announcements through various mediums and providing information in many different languages will help parents plan for conferences. Flexibility is key in planning sessions so that parents have the option of early morning, afternoon, or early evening times, as well as the option for extended sessions. Teachers can also coordinate free services through the PTA, such as transportation, childcare, and refreshments. Two-way communication can be achieved through providing opportunities for dialogue, flexibility, and an open and receptive attitude.

In recent years, there has been a trend toward student-led parent-teacher conferences. The rationale behind this method holds that when students step up as a catalyst for parent-teacher communication, students gain accountability for their educational development, awareness of the importance of open communication, and leadership skills, among other benefits. In the student-led parent-teacher conference model, teachers act as facilitators while students are responsible for answering any teacher or parent questions pertaining to academic achievement, student portfolios, educational development, and grades and assessment. Some teachers have students fill out self-assessment surveys before a conference to help students evaluate their learning, their strengths, weaknesses, skills, and habits, and their social interaction with classmates. This approach to parent-teacher conferences helps parents see their children taking initiative for their own educational process, and helps to transfer that open communication during conferences to the home environment.

Administrative duties

The responsibilities of a music educator include more than just designing and implementing a music curriculum; they also include the logistical aspects of running a music program. Music educators must be able to balance the budget allotted for the music program through the school. This involves buying and maintaining the appropriate number of instruments and music materials needed for the students without exceeding the program funds. Accurate and thorough bookkeeping combined with a strategic view of inventory maintenance will help a music educator maintain a healthy budget. Music educators must log inventory and keep track of all materials and instruments. Administrative duties also include scheduling student rehearsals, practices, lessons, contests, conferences, and performances. Music educators can use scheduling programs for better organization and delegate students' own scheduling. Contests, conferences, and performances should be planned well ahead of a season's start date so that educators can plan promotional materials, marketing, and performance curriculum.

Minimizing financial cost of a music program

Music programs in the current decade face many financial challenges within school districts; when faced with budget cuts, music programs must find ways to minimize the financial impact of their annual operating costs. Loaning music from other programs or libraries can reduce spending on new scores and music. Some movie theaters screen performances of operas, symphonies, and other concerts at a lower cost than a live theater performance. Consider distributing course materials electronically when possible, as printing costs that may seem small in isolation will accumulate over the course of a year. In a program that provides instruments that will be shared among students, ensure regular maintenance and instrument care to prevent damages that can mean expensive repair or replacements. A director should attempt to design performances and outreach efforts in a way that will create value for the community, while creating political and financial support for the school.

Factors affecting student participation in a school music program

Outcomes in a student's musical education are the result of a complex interaction of a large variety of variables, both genetic and environmental. The strongest factors impeding positive outcomes are those associated with poverty. Hunger, physical and emotional abuse, and chronic illness can lead to poor school performance, and health-risk behaviors are consistently linked with poor grades and test scores and lower educational attainment. School health programs have been shown to reduce health-risk behaviors and have a positive effect on academic achievement. Supportive teacher-student relationships have also been shown to positively affect social and academic outcomes for students, enabling them to feel secure in the learning environment. Students in high-poverty urban schools may benefit even more than their high-income counterparts from positive teacher-student relationships, given the strong association between poverty and negative outcomes.

Mechanisms of a simple sound system

A simple sound system used for sound amplification consists of an input transducer, signal processing, and an output transducer. The input transducer can take the form of a microphone, which converts the sound that is picked up into audio signals that travel down cables to the signal processor. A signal processor can take the form of a mixing console through which the audio signals are processed in three ways. First, the audio signal goes through a preamplification system in which the sound that is picked up is amplified up to line level. Then, the audio signal goes through an equalizer in which an audio engineer or console operator adjusts the specific levels of tone quality for the most aesthetically pleasing balance. If necessary, the audio signal undergoes mixing, in which multiple inputs are processed together into one line-level output signal. The output transducer can take the form of a loudspeaker, and the single line-level output signal is amplified and converted back into sound.

Proper microphone technique for vocal amplification

When singing into a microphone, a singer may have immaculate vocal technique but still not sound ideal. Vocal amplification requires proper microphone technique to maximize the aesthetic balance of a loudspeaker. A good sound starts with an ideal fit between the voice and the microphone. A high-pitched voice would fit with a microphone that adds warmth through the mid and low ranges, whereas a deeper and darker voice would fit better with a microphone that lightens the sound with treble and upper-mid prominence. Also, the singer should sing into the center of the microphone, not across the top or at a wrong angle. The singer should not strain to sing into the microphone, but should think of the microphone as an extension of the ears. Singers should sing at a consistent distance away from the microphone, to ensure maximal sound pick-up. If there is a sudden increase in singing volume, however, the singer should back away slightly so as not to blast the sound system.

MIDI technology

MIDI stands for Musical Instrument Digital Interface and provides a standard "language" of MIDI that allows communication between digital keyboards, computers, and even cell phones. MIDI does not record a digital version of a sound recording, but instead stores performance data of a particular performance. MIDI data includes tempo settings, which notes are to be played, what rhythms are to be played, which instruments are to be played, and the volume levels of the instruments. Since the recorded data are inherently performance instructions, MIDI-stored performances can be changed to sound on different instruments, in different keys, and in different tempi. MIDI technology has become a staple in the music industry, with its simplicity of recording, compact storage size, and multitude of practical applications in recording, editing, and performing.

DAW

DAW stands for Digital Audio Workstation and is a computer-based recording, sequencing, and mixing tool for the modern musician. A complete DAW includes the computer, the digital audio software, a digital audio interface, optional plug-ins, digital signal processing, and possibly additional digital audio interfaces. It is important to choose the right digital sequencing software to have the right tools where needed. Avid Pro Tools is a popular DAW software and has become the standard in recording studios and home studios as well. MOTU Digital Performer is one of the oldest DAWs around and is compatible with both Mac and Windows. Apple Logic Pro is also one of the top DAWs and provides a wealth of interface options but is compatible with Apple products only. Ableton Live is one of the best live recording DAWs and offers many third-party hardware options made especially for the program. FL Studio is a classic DAW for creating loop- and sample-based music.

Classroom computer for music use

A classroom computer in any music room proves to be an invaluable resource for the twenty-first century music student. With the music technology at hand, a classroom computer can help to reinforce lesson materials, provide a launching pad for music technology instruction, and offer students a wide array of resources for making music. The classroom computer should have enough RAM and storage to run multimedia programs, be Internet-ready, and have audio input and output features, speakers, and a CD- or DVD-ROM player. The computer should have easy-to-use menu screens and controls so that the students can easily navigate through the programs. The computer should have loudspeakers as well as headphones. The computer should also include MIDI, notation, and sequencing software, as well as electronic instruments with which to experiment and create sound in the DAW software.

Notation software

Notation software provides an important tool in music education, allowing students to notate compositions electronically, transfer the data to other MIDI instruments, and integrate technology into the music classroom. Using notation software helps to reinforce musical concepts and compositional lessons for the students. Many notation programs will transcribe the music as it is played on an attached keyboard or sung into a microphone. Notes can also be manually input by the mouse. The premier notation software Sibelius features high ease of use, varied input/output capabilities, great editing options, and good technical support. Finale is another widely used notation software and features student versions as well as professional versions. MagicScore Maestro features easy notational input, but does not have controls that are as intuitive as other notation software. Forte Home is a great notation software for the beginner but features no virtual piano.

Inputting music into desktop music publishing software

There are various methods of inputting music into desktop music publishing software. Many programs will notate the music as played by a MIDI instrument such as a keyboard or guitar. Some programs can also notate music that is sung into a microphone. This method allows the most organic processing from live music to notation, but may require some cleaning up after the music has been notated into the program. Another way of inputting music into desktop music publishing software is by manually placing each note and rest through the mouse. This method allows for more meticulous control of each note placement, but can be highly time-consuming. Some desktop music publishing software can process scanned print music into the proper notational format within the software. This method is highly efficient for multiple pages of sheet music, but will have to be cleaned once the scanned music has been transferred into the program.

Finale, Nightingale, and Overture

Finale is one of the most widely used notation software packages on the market. It allows music to be input through MIDI-controlled instruments as well as through scanning, and then converts the data onto a staff. Finale features a diverse playback instrument library and allows easy sharing between users. Tools like transposition, range checking, production, and sequencing capabilities make Finale an essential tool for the musician. Nightingale notation software is available on the Mac platform only, and offers a simple, basic approach to digital notation. Nightingale offers a PostScript output equal to that of other notation software, with similar features such as MIDI and scanning input, as well as playback, transposition, and orchestration tools. Overture is highly intuitive notation software that features many similar tools such as MIDI and scanning input and diverse editing options, but also includes VST, Virtual Studio Technology, which allows ease of integration between software audio synthesizers, plug-ins, Overture, and other recording systems.

Filtering software for music classrooms

Filtering software is one method to protect students from obscene, inappropriate, and otherwise harmful websites on the Internet. The filtering software can be set to a variety of levels, from most restrictive to least restrictive. Even at the least restrictive setting, the software blocks pornographic content, obscene subject matter, and other inappropriate websites. The more restrictive settings marginally block more content, but may also block safe educational content through unreliable and inconsistent measures. Some educators have voiced opposition to filtering software, claiming inconsistent and unreliable results, interference of legitimate education websites, and a lack of input across the school district. Opposition also claims that filtering software prevents students from learning how to make their own sound decisions based on real-world knowledge. Despite the challenges of filtering software, it is still a necessary tool in providing a safe and positive learning environment for students.

Music license

Under the 1976 Copyright Act, music teachers are exempt from copyright recording laws only if they make a single copy of a student performance of a copyrighted work for educational purposes or for documentation. If a teacher makes duplicates of the recording, then a music license is necessary. In this case, a licensing fee is required for each copy of the recording that is duplicated and distributed. Music educators must contact the Harry Fox Agency to acquire the correct music license for distribution. The licensee must pay a fee to the copyright holder of 9.1 cents per song that is five minutes or shorter, or 1.75 cents for every minute or fraction of the song that exceeds five minutes. This licensing fee applies to each copyrighted work. Although festivals and recording companies may pay royalty fees, it is ultimately the music educator's responsibility to ensure that all royalties are paid to prevent undue consequences from copyright law enforcement.

Instructional Emphasis: Choral

Classical singing timbre vs. popular music timbre

Both classical and popular vocal music traditions strive to create a beautiful sound through singing. However, because of differing aesthetics, the two different traditions hold many different vocal techniques. In classical singing, the mouth cavity is trained to have a high palate as in a yawn to create an open, formal sound. In popular singing, there is much more flexibility to the shape of the mouth, and many singers use both high and low palates to manipulate the different vocal sounds. Classical singers are encouraged to use a rich, wide vibrato to add to the color of the singing tone, while popular singers use less vibrato in their songs. Also, classical singers focus on producing pure vowel tones and clear consonants, while popular singers use a wide variety of sounds, timbres, and techniques such as the rasp, growl, and edge, to achieve emotional range.

Classically trained voice

The register of a voice refers to a range of pitches that have a similar tonal quality produced by similar vocal production. In singing, there are three general registers: for men, they are typically the chest, head, and falsetto; for women, they are called the chest, middle, and head voices. The chest register refers to the lower ranges of the voice and are said to have a heavier tonal quality similar to that of the natural talking voice. The head voice, or the middle voice for women, refers to the upper ranges of the voice and is said to have a lighter tonal quality that is not falsetto. Falsetto, or the head voice for women, refers to the highest ranges of the voice above the normal speaking voice and is said to have a breathy, fairy tonal quality that lacks a lot of overtones.

Physiological mechanisms of singing

When using the voice as an instrument, it is important to understand the physiological mechanisms involved in producing sound. The three main vocal parts involved in creating sound are the air supply, vibrator, and resonator. Air supply is taken into the lungs by the inspiratory muscles, especially the diaphragm, and emptied from the lungs by the expiratory muscles. The vibrators for singing are the vocal folds, held within the voice box or larynx at the top of the trachea. When air passes through the vocal folds through the opening called the glottis, the vocal folds vibrate and produce sound. The sound passes through the resonators, principally the pharynx and the mouth cavities. These resonators influence the tonal quality of the sound through the cavity shapes and surfaces, as well as the various singing techniques used to alter sound and timbre.

Correct use of breath for singing

For any singer, the breath plays an essential role in producing a controlled, robust tone while keeping the vocal chords in good health. To begin any breath, the singer must inhale first; the inhalation should be deep and initiated by the contraction of the diaphragm, the muscle and tendon that runs along the bottom of the ribcage. As the diaphragm contracts and is actively engaged, it creates a vacuum in the lungs, which begins the intake of oxygen. After the intentional inhalation, the singer must control the rate of exhalation, as the flow of air through the vocal chords results in sound. The singer must use great care not to allow the chest to collapse while managing the rate of airflow by engaging the abdominal muscles to achieve a steady stream of air through the trachea and larynx.

Breathing warm-up

Before beginning any choral rehearsal, it is essential for the director to prepare the singers both physically and mentally. One important aspect of warming up a choral ensemble is the breathing warm-up. Breathing warm-ups engage the diaphragm for supported singing and help to warm the vocal chords for singing. Not only will the breathing exercises physically prepare the lungs and vocal mechanisms for singing, they will also mentally center the singer to be mindful of breath during the rehearsal. One choral breathing warm-up consists of taking in a deep breath over as many counts as possible, holding the breath, and then slowly letting out the air on an "s" sound, over as many counts as possible. Another choral warm-up consists of having the singers exhale on a pulse with an open mouth "ha."

Vocalization warm-ups

Before beginning any choral rehearsal, it is essential for the director to prepare the singers both physically and mentally through vocalization warm-ups. One such warm-up is the siren, in which all the singers sing to the upper reaches of their vocal range and slide back down to their lower reaches. Another warm-up consists of singing pentatonic scales upwards and downwards using consonant- and vowel-heavy sentences such as "Mommy Made Me Mash My M&Ms." Choruses can also warm up by sliding their voices from a Do to a Sol and back down. Yet another warm-up consists of singing Do to the next Do an octave up, back down to Sol-Mi-Do. A warm-up useful for vowels consists of singing a single pitch through the five vowels from open to close, or vice versa: "ee," "eh," "ah," "oh," and "oo."

Physical warm-ups

Before beginning any choral rehearsal, it is essential for the director to prepare the singers both physically and mentally. The use of physical warm-ups helps the body to release any tension that may hinder the vocal delivery while also increasing blood flow to the vocal mechanisms. A useful physical warm-up to prepare the lips for singing consists of taking in a deep breath and releasing it through slack lips, as in a lip trill. Another helpful warm-up to prepare the mouth for singing consists of stretching the mouth wide open while imitating the chewing motion. Singers must also stretch appropriately before singing to help loosen the neck and shoulder muscles through shoulder rolls, neck rolls, side bends, and arm extensions. Singers can also take in deep breaths, and release them as heavy sighs while dropping the shoulders to help loosen the body.

Ideal posture

The ideal posture for singing should engage the entire body while avoiding any tension or restrictions on the vocal mechanisms. The feet should be shoulder-width apart, with one foot slightly in front of the other for optimal balance. The weight of the body should lean slightly forward instead of backwards on the heels. The knees should be loose and never locked. The hands should be relaxed and kept by the side of the body or engaged in expressing a vocal line. The abdomen should be active and involved in supporting the breath. The arms and shoulders should be relaxed and allowed to hang freely. The chest should not be collapsed, but should be held high to support the breath. The singer's chin should be held level to the floor so as not to obstruct the flow of air through the trachea.

When singing, it is imperative to execute a healthy, proper singing posture not only for better ease in creating resonant sounds, but also for the health of the body. When the singer is standing, the weight of the body should be distributed evenly to all sides of the feet – front, back, side, and middle. The spine should be erect with the shoulders back and the neck held high. The head should not angle forward or backward, but should be kept in a neutral position so that airflow through the body has no restrictions, and so the singer's body does not sustain unnecessary fatigue. When the singer is sitting, the feet should be flat on the ground with the spine erect and aligned with the neck, shoulders, head, and ears. The body should be balanced and relaxed through the entire vocal session.

Solfège in kinesthetic pitch learning

Solfège, also known as solfeggio in Italian, originated in the seventeenth century as a vocal exercise using solmization syllables for singing the pitches of a scale. Solmization systems were found all around the world, but the most commonly used one in Western culture stems from the Guidonian system of the eleventh century. In teaching pitch names and associations, the use of solfège can greatly aid the student's understanding of high and low pitch, as educators such as John Curwen and Zoltan Kodàly have integrated a kinesthetic system using both hand signs and spatial reasoning. The solmization for the diatonic scale, from tonic to tonic, is as follows: do, re, mi, fa, sol, la, si (ti), do. As each pitch rises, the corresponding hand sign also rises from the low on the body to high above the head. The spatial, kinesthetic association allows the learner to relate the rising pitch to rising motion.

Lifting the palate

The soft palate, also called the velum, is the soft tissue at the top of the mouth cavity that rises and lowers as the mouth swallows and in speech. The soft palate is responsible for closing off the nasal cavity while the mouth swallows so that any material in the oral cavity proceeds to the esophagus. In vocal technique, singers practice singing with an open throat where the velum is raised and the larynx is lowered. This allows the sound quality to be more relaxed and free while also easing register transitions and maintaining the health of the vocal mechanisms. When singers lift the soft palate, the resulting space within the oral cavity enlarges, helping to achieve a more resonant, warm tone without restrictions. Since this action also relaxes the surrounding vocal muscles, the singer can transition between registers more easily, resulting in a consistently smooth tone.

Vowel uniformity

Vowel uniformity is an important aspect of singing, but within a chorus setting, it becomes all the more important, as there are a multitude of various timbres, ranges, and singers contributing, ideally, to a unified, homogenous sound. Each singer should practice certain vocal techniques to assist in keeping each vowel sound as uniform as possible. The mouth should be open long instead of wide, with the jaw falling low to open the oral cavity. The resulting vowels will be more open and resonant for better choral blend. The singers should also sing with an open throat while lifting the soft palate for a more relaxed and smoother sound. Also, the singer should not "swallow" his or her sound, but should direct the sound forward in the head so that the chorus can achieve a uniform, vibrant sound.

Resonance

For a singer, resonance plays an important role in enabling the voice to "carry," with a more vibrant and rich sound. Acoustically, the sound originates through the passing of air through the vibrating vocal chords; this movement creates the frequency or pitch that the audience hears. As the sound moves from the vocal chords through the vocal tract, the specific sound properties such as vowels and other resonating properties are created. The vocal tract has optimal resonances for certain frequencies, and it is important for the singer to maximize the resonances of the vibrating vocal tract with the specific pitch frequencies. For this reason, many sopranos will maximize vocal tract resonance at high frequencies by creating more space in the oral cavity and relaxing the vocal tract so that the resultant sound is vibrant and sonorous.

Blocked section, mixed, and column choral formations

In a choral blocked section, the vocal parts are solidly separated from front to back so all sopranos are grouped at one end from front row to back row, altos are grouped next to them from front to back, tenors are grouped next to the altos from front to back, and basses bring up the other end from front to back. The choral sound from a blocked formation tends to be better suited for homophonic pieces, but can create issues of the singers being able to listen to other parts. In a choral columnar section, the vocal parts are separated in columns, with tenors behind the sopranos, and basses behind the altos. A column formation suits polyphonic music, as it is easier for singers to hear for balance. In a mixed formation, the sopranos, altos, tenors, and basses are individually alternating in SATB pattern. A mixed formation is good for intonation and the mixing of sound at the audience, but may require more training in singing independently.

Physiology of vocal range development

Until puberty, a child's vocal mechanisms are not fully developed and do not contain the full range of the adult voice. Infants are born with a very high larynx; the larynx drops slightly when a child reaches the age of three. From age three until about age 10-13, the larynx is not yet fully functional. The vocal folds of a child are much shorter than an adult's vocal folds, and the larynx of a child sits higher than an adult's. The vocal range of a child is relatively limited as compared to an adult; high and low pitches are reached by the lengthening or thickening of the vocal folds. During puberty, a child's larynx grows to its full size, drops, and the vocal chords lengthen and thicken substantially. The fully matured vocal mechanisms acquire a vocal range much larger than a child's, functioning through the complex muscular and cartilage actions within the larynx to produce wide-ranging pitches in different registers.

Repertoire sources

Choral directors should choose intermediate middle school choir repertoire that is of high quality, teachable, and appropriate for the range, ability level, cultural context, and programming considerations of the ensemble. There are many repertoire sources for the middle school choral director that can assist in preliminary repertoire selections. The American Choral Directors Association publishes multiple repertoire lists including "Tried and True Literature" for junior high choirs, as well as annual honor choir repertoire lists. Donald Roach's *Complete Secondary Choral Music Guide* includes extensive repertoire lists, music theater sources, and other content that is valuable for the middle school choral director. Music directors can also consult state clinic and contest repertoire lists. Several publishing companies also produce suggested repertoire for intermediate choirs as well as complete compilations of choral works for the middle school choir.

Bright tone vs. a dark tone

"Bright" and "dark" are descriptions of tonal quality. Tonal quality is independent from pitch, as demonstrated by a violin and a cello, for example. If both were played to produce the same note, their tonal qualities would still differ, with the violin producing a brighter tone. A bright tone emphasizes the partials in the upper midrange. A dark tone, in contrast, will have a tonal balance emphasizing the lower range, with weak high frequencies. In terms of singing, a bright tone is one that resonates farther forward in the face, and is associated with the front vowels [i] and [e]. A dark tone resonates further back, and is associated with the vowels [u], [o], and [a]. In a full chorus, the brightness or darkness of a passage can be adjusted through the manipulation of vowel quality. In general, female vocalists will tend to have brighter tones.

Intonation and vocal technique

A fundamental element of good choral sound lies in accurate intonation. Without all of the voices sounding in pitch, balance and blend become the least of a choral director's concerns. There are many rehearsal techniques to improve a chorus' intonation. Sometimes, changing the seating arrangement of the chorus can drastically improve intonation. Be sure that all vocal parts can hear each other clearly so that intonation is no longer an issue. If the seating arrangement is not the issue, then the director can take the singers through a problem spot singing every beat vertically, stopping on each harmony for accurate pitches. Directors can also warm up with dominant chords and tonic pedals so that the singers always have a reference pitch to tune to. Singers should practice breathing exercises, vocalizations, and etudes to strengthen their vocal mechanisms and their overall vocal technique.

Tongue

The tongue plays a key role in vowel formation and clear diction, as it directly influences the vocal tract and the larynx. With all other vocal mechanisms fixed, a change in the tongue directly changes the vocal sound, from dull and distorted to tinny and harsh. Clarity in singing requires clear vowel formation for the words to be intelligible to the listening audience. For clear vowels, the tongue should rest forward in the mouth, with the tip of the tongue resting against the bottom teeth for the most space in the mouth for resonance. The back of the tongue should not press against the throat, but should be kept away from the throat for clear and unobstructed delivery of airflow and sound. The tongue should always be kept relaxed and free from tension when singing, to avoid a choked sound and possible injury to the vocal mechanisms.

Diaphragm

The diaphragm plays a central role in the respiratory system, as one of the main acting forces behind inhalation and exhalation. The diaphragm is a sheet of muscle that separates the abdomen from the chest cavity. The diaphragm muscle is attached to the lower parts of the rib cage, the spine, and the lower edge of the sternum. As the muscle contracts, it increases the length and diameter of the chest cavity, causing a vacuum in the lungs, inducing air to enter the lungs through inhalation. During exhalation, the diaphragm muscle naturally relaxes, deflating the lungs and expelling the air out from the lungs. When singing, it is important to actively engage the diaphragm during inhalation for a deep supported breath, as well as during exhalation to prolong the supported singing breath as long as possible.

Symptoms of adolescent vocal change and techniques

As students undergo puberty, hormonal fluctuations and growth spurts cause many singers the added challenges of adolescent vocal change. Females typically undergo puberty between the ages of 10 and18, while males typically undergo puberty between the ages of 12 and20. Adolescent vocal change occurs in both males and females, but is most prominent in male singers. During puberty, the vocal tract increases in length and circumference, and the larynx increases in size and density. Symptoms include cracking and abrupt register breaks. While the vocal mechanisms are developing in adolescent students, it is important to practice safe and intelligent techniques of singing rather than pushing the vocal mechanisms to damage. The body should be both energetic and relaxed, providing proper support for the breath but never pushing. Equally important during this developmental stage is proper rest for the singing voice; students should never sing too loud or with too much effort, which could injure the vocal mechanisms.

Tessitura

Tessitura refers to that range within a singer's vocal abilities that resonate the most in an aesthetically pleasing manner. The particular tessitura of a singer's voice type is also usually the most comfortable for his or her vocal timbre. Tessitura differs from vocal range in that the range of a singer's voice refers to the limits of pitches the singer is able to sing; the tessitura of a singer's voice, although he or she may have a wide singing range, may be best described as a high tessitura, or a low tessitura, wherever the voice is able to sustain the most dramatic, comfortable, and pleasing sound. When assigning a voice to a vocal part, it is important to consider the tessitura of a particular voice as well as his or her range, timbre, transition points, and voice weight.

Instructional Emphasis: Instrumental

Brass instruments

Brass instruments typically produce sound through the buzzing of the player's lips as the air travels through a tubular, expanding metallic wind instrument. The lips act as a vibrating valve that produces oscillating air and pressure. As the air vibrates through the tubular instrument, some of the energy is lost as viscous and thermal energy, while the rest emerges from the instrument as sound. Almost all brass instruments consist of a tube that gets larger towards the end of the tube called the bell. The tube is often coiled so that the instrument is easier for the player to hold. Brass instruments resonate at certain frequencies more easily than others, so to produce other tones, players can change the length of the instruments through valves or slides. Narrower, more cylindrical brass instruments like the trumpet and the trombone produce sharp and clear sounds, while wider, larger-belled brass instruments like the French horn and euphonium produce warmer, darker sounds.

Dynamics for the brass instruments are a product of the volume of air moving through the instrument, sometimes referred to as velocity. Since sound is produced in brass instruments through the buzzing of the player's lips, careful attention must be placed on lip technique when performing dynamic changes, due to the interaction of embouchure and the breath. The tendency of a pitch when moving in the direction of piano to forte, if the embouchure remains steady, is for the pitch to bend sharp, or even to move to the next pitch "shelf" due to the increase in velocity. The opposite is also true: at lower dynamic ranges, the player must decrease airflow velocity, which requires additional support through the diaphragm as well as a tighter embouchure, or else the pitch will fall flat.

For brass instruments, proper brass embouchure and good air support directly affect tone quality. The player must provide consistent breath support through deep inhalations, controlled exhalations, and a relaxed body. Once the player has a good breath foundation, proper embouchure must also be practiced for tone quality, intonation, endurance, range, and articulation. For the brass player, the lips are the source of a sound wave's motion and energy; the mouth cavity should be wide and open while the lips touch together as if saying "M." When the player buzzes, the lips should stay relaxed while the corners of the lips should stay firm, not too tight or too loose. The player should keep the chin even and pointed. As a general guideline, the player should keep the mouthpiece equally held between the two lips.

Brass instruments include those wind instruments that are typically made with metal and sounded by the vibration of the player's lips through a mouthpiece. The French horn is typically notated on the treble or bass clefs sounded a perfect fifth lower with a general range of F#2-C6. The trumpet is typically notated on the treble clef with the C trumpet sounding as written and the Bb trumpet sounding a major second higher, both with a general range of F#3-D6. The tenor trombone is typically notated on the bass, tenor, or alto clefs sounding as written, with a general range of E2-F5. The bass trombone is typically notated on the bass clef sounding as written, with a general range of Bb1-Bb4. The tuba is typically notated on the bass clef sounding as written, with a general range of G0-C5. The euphonium is typically notated on the bass or treble clefs sounding as written on the bass clef or a major ninth lower on the treble clef, with a general range of Bb1-F5.

Correct intonation on brass instruments is the result of properly forming the entire system flowing from the diaphragm to the end of the instrument. Playing with good posture and breath support allows the player to play at a wide variety of registers and volumes more comfortably, reducing strained intonation that can occur at extremes. Cue the student to think of the airway from the lungs to the throat and the oral cavity as a broad and open passageway. Playing in front of a mirror allows the student to monitor horn placement and embouchure. Mental practice is extremely important. The student should have a clear idea of the tone she wants to produce, and think actively about playing with good tone. Long tones are an excellent tool for developing intonation. Depending on the particular instrument, the student should learn which note fingerings are inherently out of tune and how to adjust the relevant slide to compensate.

Brass instruments require care and maintenance on several fronts. Instruments should always be handled with care. Avoid handling the finish and wipe away any oil, dirt, or other debris with a soft cloth after handling. Be careful to avoid any damage from jewelry, buttons, or zippers. Before storage, use a swab to remove as much moisture as possible from the inside of the instrument, and remove the mouthpiece before storage. For valved instruments, apply a small amount of valve oil before each playing session. Clean and lubricate all slides, removing old lubricant before applying a new layer, and use only a small amount, removing any excess with a soft cloth. Whenever possible, keep the instrument in a cool environment that is neither too dry nor too humid. Perform a regular inspection of all moving parts and the mouthpiece

Keyboard instruments

Keyboard instruments include those instruments whose sound-producing mechanisms are set into motion through a system of levers and keys. The keyboard is generally made up of seven natural and five chromatic keys. The distance between the natural keys are whole steps except for the half steps between E-F and B-C. The modern piano is typically notated on the grand staff sounding as written, with a general range of A0-C8. The celesta is typically notated on the grand staff sounding an octave higher, with a general range of C3-C7. The harpsichord is typically notated on the grand staff sounding as written, with a general range of F1-F6. The harmonium is typically notated on the grand staff sounding as written, with a general range of F1-F6. The organ is typically notated on the grand staff sounding as written, with a general range of C2-C7.

When executing finger technique on keyboard instruments, one must always be aware of relaxed wrists, arms, elbows, and shoulders to prevent overuse injuries. The wrist should be held in line with the hand and the arm, not sagging or raised too high. The elbows should hang comfortably to the side of the body and never tensed. The shoulders should be relaxed and dropped and never raised, as this is a sign of tension. Fingering at the keyboard should use the thumb-tuck technique, to allow a flowing and continuous line of notes when playing. When tucking the thumb under the middle or ring fingers, the keyboardist should ensure that the wrist does not drop during the movement, but that the thumb helps to maintain a healthy wrist position. Players should always drill a fingering section slowly at first, and only increase the playing speed if the passage can be executed without tension.

When the keyboardist plays an octave passage in either or both hands, the hand is required to stretch to the length of eight keys. The motion should be played and released quickly since the reach of the octave can present unnecessary tension and exhaustion to the arm if not released quickly. One school of thought has the hand play an octave quickly, but releasing the tension as quickly as possible back to a neutral hand position. In a long passage of octave playing, this method requires the quick stretch and release at each octave. Another school of thought has the hand fixed in an octave position and uses the quick movement of a flexible wrist snapping for each motion to play the octave passage as quickly as possible. Yet another school of thought has the hand and wrist fixed in the octave position and uses the quick movement of the elbow to play each octave.

Orff instruments

Regular care and maintenance of Orff instruments helps to prolong the life of the instruments. Music educators can involve students in the care and maintenance of the instruments for a learned sense of responsibility as well as an efficient method of cleaning the instruments. Music educators can provide an end-of-the-year event that includes the cleaning of all Orff instruments. Students should remove the instrument bars and start with the vacuuming of all dust from the instrument. Next, the students should take a damp rag with an oil soap to wash and clean the boxes and wooden bars. After the instrument has been cleaned, the students can then take an oil polish such as common furniture polish to keep the instrument in proper, working condition. Music teachers can also have the students place a sticky note on any broken pins for the teacher to replace.

Percussion instruments

Percussion instruments are instruments that produce sound by being hit, scraped, or shaken. Certain percussion instruments such as drums produce sound through the vibration of a membrane around a resonating body. Also known as membranophones, the membrane on these instruments can be struck by hands or mallets, as well as rubbed and scraped. Other percussion instruments produce vibrations without the aid of air, string, or membranes; these musical instruments are known as idiophones and include concussion idiophones, percussion idiophones, rattles, scrapers, and friction idiophones. Concussion idiophones are two objects that are struck together; examples include rhythm sticks, castanets, and claves. Percussion idiophones are those struck by mallets and include marimbas, bells, gongs, and xylophones. Rattles are shaken, such as a maraca. Scrapers are stroked across a notched surface, such as washboards and guiros. Friction idiophones are played by rubbing and include the musical saw and the glass harmonica.

Pitched percussion instruments can include membranophones as well as idiophones that have definite pitches. The timpani is typically notated in bass clef sounding as written with the 30-inch timpani in a range of D2-A2, the 28-inch timpani in a range of F2-C3, the 25-inch timpani in a range of Bb2-F3, and the 23-inch timpani in a range of D3-A3. The xylophone is typically notated in treble clef sounding an octave higher, with a general range of G4-C7. The marimba is typically notated on the grand staff sounding as written, with a general range of C2 or A2 to C7. The glockenspiel is typically notated in treble clef sounding two to eight octaves higher, with a general range of G3-C6. The vibraphone is typically notated in treble clef sounding as written, with a general range of F3-F6. Chimes are typically notated in treble clef sounding an octave higher, with a general range of C4-G5.

Percussion instruments require regular maintenance and inspection depending on the specific percussion instrument involved. Timpanis should be regularly inspected for an even and smooth head with a balanced action. The rim should be greased regularly with lubricant such as cork grease, and the tension screws should be oiled regularly with lug lubricants. Make sure to keep the timpani covered when not in use. Mallet instruments should be wiped regularly with a glass cleaner, and special attention should be made to keep the resonators clean. Frequent inspections should be made to ensure that there are no splintered or cracked bars that need to be replaced. Drums should also be maintained regularly through the cleaning and lubricating of the hardware. Periodically inspect the rim, counterhoop, and head for any serious issues that would warrant repair or replacement.

Stringed instruments

Stringed instruments produce sound through the vibrations of the strings on a resonating body usually made of wood. The strings, made of nylon, steel, or silk, can be set in motion by plucking, bowing, or striking. As the string sets the surrounding air in motion, it also vibrates the soundboard through the bridge as the resonant vibrator and the audible tone effuses out of the instrument through a sound hole. Pitches on a stringed instrument are modified by string tension, thickness, and length: the higher the tension, the higher the pitch; the thicker the string, the lower the pitch; and the longer the string, the lower the pitch. Strings can be parallel to the soundboard as in the lute, guitar, violin, piano, and dulcimer, or at a right angle to the soundboard as in the harp.

On a stringed instrument, many techniques can be applied to produce dynamic changes. When playing with a bow, the variables that affect dynamics are the speed and pressure of the bow. When playing louder dynamics such as forte, fortissimo, and mezzo forte, the bow must move faster across the strings with greater pressure to produce greater amplitudes in the vibrating sound waves. When playing softer dynamics such as piano, mezzo piano, and pianissimo, the bow moves a little slower across the strings with less pressure to produce smaller amplitudes in the vibrating sound waves. When stringed instruments are plucked, this is often notated in the score as pizzicato. When plucking a stringed instrument, the sound produced has a sharper attack; dynamic changes are produced similarly: a heavier pluck at greater speed increases dynamics, while a softer, slower pluck diminishes the dynamics.

String instruments include those instruments whose main vibrating system is a string set into motion by plucking, striking, or bowing. The violin is typically notated in the treble clef sounding as written, with a general range of G3-A7. The viola is typically notated in the alto clef sounding as written, with a general range of C3-E6. The cello is typically notated in the bass, tenor, and treble clefs sounding as written, with a general range of C2-C6. The double bass is typically notated in bass clef sounding an octave lower, with a general range of C2-C5. The banjo is typically notated in treble clef sounding as written, with a general range of C3-A4. The guitar is typically notated in treble clef sounding an octave lower, with a general range of E3-E6. The harp is typically notated on the grand staff sounding as written, with a general range of Cb1-G#7.

The bow position on a violin and viola should have a rounded thumb holding the side of the bow with a pinky on top of the bow, with the other fingers comfortably holding the other side of the bow. The fingers should be fairly arched during a down stroke and more elongated during an up stroke. The bow should not be held with any tension but firmly and lightly. The player should be careful not to extend any finger, as this will create tension in the wrist. On the cello and bass, the bow should be held in a similar manner to both the violin and viola bow, but the pinky finger does not rest on top of the bow; instead, the pinky should rest next to the middle and ring fingers. Since both the cello and bass are played upright, the arm does not generally stay above the bow; in fact, bow handling on a cello and bass requires the elbow and arm to lower significantly whether playing near the tip of the bow or near the frog.

Stringed instruments require care and maintenance on several fronts. The instrument should be handled with care, and players should avoid directly handling the fragile varnish, which can be damaged by oils on the hands. When playing, care should be taken to avoid damage by jewelry, buttons, or zippers. Immediately after each use, remove oil, rosin dust, and other debris with a soft cloth. Special treated cloths can be used, but must not be used on strings or the hair of the bow. String instruments should, whenever possible, be kept in a well-regulated environment away from excessive exposure to direct light, too hot or too cold temperatures, and too dry or too humid environments. Failure to observe these precautions can result in bending, cracking, glue joint separations, arching distortion, and many other problems.

Woodwind instruments

Woodwind instruments produce sound through vibrations in an enclosed tube. The vibrations can be set into motion by blowing through single or double reeds, across an opening, or through an opening. Single-reed woodwind instruments produce sound when air is blown through a reed that vibrates against the mouthpiece. Single-reed instruments include the clarinet and the saxophone. Double-reed woodwind instruments produce sound when air is blown through two reeds that are tied together and vibrate. Double-reed instruments include the oboe, bassoon, and sarrusophone. Woodwinds that produce sound when the player blows across an opening are the transverse flutes, which are held sideways. Woodwinds that produce sound when the player blows directly into an opening are the whistle and the recorder. Players change the pitch of an instrument by shortening or lengthening the air column through covered holes or keys.

Warming up serves several important physical and mental functions for the wind instrumentalist. Mentally, it has the effect of centering and adjusting the player to an appropriate mental state for performance and establishing proper physiological cues for posture, breathing, etc., before performance. In addition to establishing the mindset for performance, the warm-up provides necessary functions at a physical level. The warm-up promotes blood flow to the fingers and the structures associated with embouchure, making them feel "loose" and ready to respond to the demands of playing. Though easy to overlook, the warm-up serves an important function for the instrument as well as the body. An instrument that has been sitting in an air-conditioned room is significantly colder than it will be during a performance. The warm air of the player's breath passing through the instrument will create warmth and thus expansion. An instrument should either be warm before tuning or re-tuned after a thorough warm-up.

Woodwind instruments include single reeds, double reeds, and flutes. All woodwind instruments have side holes that are left open or covered to change the sounding length of the tube. The piccolo is typically notated on the treble clef an octave lower and has a general range of D4-C7. The flute is typically notated on the treble clef with no transposition, and has a general range of Bb3-D7. The oboe is typically notated on the treble clef with no transposition and has a general range of Bb3-A6. The clarinet is typically notated on the treble clef with the Bb clarinet sounding a major second lower, the A clarinet sounding a minor third lower, the D clarinet sounding a major second higher, the Eb clarinet sounding a minor third higher, and all with a general range of E3-C7. The bassoon is typically notated on the bass or tenor clefs with no transposition and has a general range of Bb1-Eb5.

The reed interacts with the player's airflow and vibrations against the body of the instrument in four ways that influence the tone and sound. A reed's response refers to the ability of the reed to maintain a high quality of sound through all registers without splattering or spreading. The reed's resistance refers to the amount of embouchure tension required to keep the reed behaving and sounding with a good tone. A reed that has a low resistance may cause the player to overblow in searching for a fuller tone, while a reed that has a high resistance can cause the player fatigue and difficulty in creating a good tone. A reed's tone quality refers to the resonance and timbre of the reed itself. A reed with only lower partials will sound dull; a reed with only higher partials will sound shrill and thin. A reed's stability refers to the ability of the reed to hold pitch at any dynamic and can influence the sound in sounding flat, stable, wild, sharp, or dull.

Correct intonation on woodwind instruments is the result of properly forming the entire system flowing from the diaphragm to the end of the instrument. Playing with good posture and breath support allows the player to play at a wide variety of registers and volumes more comfortably. Cue the student to think of the airway from the lungs to the throat and the oral cavity as a broad and open passageway. Playing in front of a mirror allows the student to monitor embouchure. The student should have a clear idea of the tone she wants to produce, and think actively about playing with good tone. Long tones are an excellent tool for developing intonation. Tuning to the rest of the ensemble, piano, or tuner should be done only after a thorough warm-up, at which point tuning adjustments to the instrument, such as pushing in or pulling out sections, can be made.

There are two types of woodwind embouchure based on the type of woodwind in question; transverse flute embouchures require the player to blow air across the instrument body, while the reed woodwind embouchure requires the player to enclose the mouthpiece so that the airflow can effectively vibrate the reed in sound production. The transverse flute should be placed against the chin so that the bottom lip is in line and close to the hole. The corners of the mouth should be relaxed, while the upper lip is held firmly against the upper teeth. On a reed woodwind, the mouthpiece should be taken into the mouth only as far as the reed meets the mouthpiece. The bottom lip should be placed slightly over the bottom teeth and against the reed. The upper teeth should rest on top of the mouthpiece while the corners of the mouth are drawn in to create a seal around the mouthpiece.

Woodwind instrument should be handled with care, taking precaution to avoid damage by jewelry, buttons, or zippers. Instruments should be kept dry while in storage. After each playing session the instrument should be wiped clean, making sure to use an appropriately sized swab; this is especially important for the small-bored piccolo and oboe. On a monthly basis, apply key oil to key pivot points. Similarly, apply a small amount of cork grease to tenons and neck corks, taking care to remove any excess grease. Wipe down the finish of the instrument to remove fingerprints and oils from fingers, moisture, and other debris. Never use alcohol on any plastic parts, and never use excessive force when constructing the instrument. Thoroughly clean out the mouth between eating and playing; clean mouthpieces weekly. For reed instruments, discard reeds that are chipped or cracked; do not leave reeds on the mouthpiece, and check metal ligatures for signs of damage, as an out-of-round ligature can damage a mouthpiece. The instrument should be kept out of direct light and excessively warm, cold, or humid environments.

Tonal characteristics of instruments

There are multiple different sound properties that make up an instrument's tone quality. First, an instrument's tone is a complex wave that is composed of many different partial frequencies; unlike a simple sine wave that has only the fundamental frequency and no partial frequencies, the sound of a complex wave will vary widely given the profile of the complex wave form, contributing greatly to the various instrumental timbres. Another sound property that affects an instrument's tone quality is the nature of the resonating body. Once the vibrations of the instrument are set into motion, the surrounding air will resonate through the instrument's body, whether it be a hollow wooden shell such as a stringed instrument or through a metal tube such a brass instrument. The resonating bodies each have their own unique set of complex resonances known as formants, further giving each instrument its own unique tone quality.

Long tones are a critical practice for brass and woodwind players. The benefit of the exercise lies in removing other aspects of performance such as reading, fingering, and so on. This allows the player to singly direct his or her focus towards the production of those aspects that create a pleasing tone. The definition of "pleasing tone" may vary according to the personal preference and the idiom of performance; however, long tones allow the performer to scrutinize and adjust pitch, timbre, vibrato, etc. Although the exercise has the additional benefit of increasing stamina and strength of the muscles involved, maximum duration of the held note should not be the sole or primary focus of long-note practice. Instead, the performer's attention should focus on the quality of the note through the coordination of the entire system that produces the note: diaphragm, throat, oral and sinus cavities, embouchure, and the instrument.

The orchestrator uses the tonal characteristics of the different instrument families to meticulously layer each sound into a collective whole. The strings tend to have a rich tonal quality and form the basis of many orchestral textures. Strings have a variety of sounds and techniques and can easily function as melody, supporting harmony, or rhythmic texture. High brasses have a clear, focused tonal quality and many times are used melodically or as a crisp rhythmic flourish. Low brasses tend to provide bass lines as well as rhythmic motives. Woodwinds have held various roles within the orchestra and can easily function as melody, supporting harmony, or rhythmic texture, similar to strings. Percussive instruments have historically held a rhythmic role in orchestral writing, but have also been used as melodic interest through the marimba, timpani, and other melodic percussion instruments.

Tuning strategies

There are a variety of tuning strategies for tuning an instrumental ensemble for rehearsal. For a beginning ensemble, the conductor may tune each student's instrument, preferably before the rehearsal starts, or quickly and efficiently at the beginning of the rehearsal. If the ensemble is at a level of playing that requires proper tuning abilities, the ensemble may tune based on the pitch of the lead oboe or lead clarinet playing the concert pitch. The conductor can also choose to have each section tune as a group at the beginning of rehearsal, so that musicians can match the pitch and timbre of the instrumental section. Also, musicians can tune based on a tuning machine that plays a pure tone concert pitch where the musicians must listen carefully to adjust their instruments to the proper pitch.

One method of tuning an ensemble starts with careful tuning upwards from the bass. In a choir, this would be the lowest bass voices; in an orchestra, this would be the basses, cellos, bass clarinets, bassoons, trombones, and tubas. In a concert band or wind ensemble, this would be the bassoons, bass clarinets, trombones, tubas, bass saxophones, and euphoniums. Once the bass instruments have been carefully and precisely tuned, the next instruments higher in range would be tuned, and so on and so forth, until the entire ensemble has been tuned through the bass, middle, and soprano ranges. The theory behind this tuning method holds that with precise tuning, the other instruments can more easily hear their tuning pitches because of the overtones and harmonics from the bass sounds. Also, the other instruments can more easily place their pitches within the context of a chord structure, as the bass becomes the foundational pitch of the ensemble.

For conductors rehearsing a beginning ensemble, helping to tune the students' instruments can save time and confusion for the students. Especially with beginner students who are still familiarizing themselves with an instrument, having help with tuning will not only save time, but also offer an opportunity to teach the student how to tune. Although tuning each student's instrument has many advantages, there are also certain disadvantages to be aware of. If possible, the conductor should tune each student's instrument before the beginning of the rehearsal; otherwise, the time taken may be inefficient and would detract from the limited rehearsal time. Also, if tuning instruments for middle school or high school students, care must be taken to encourage every student's own ability to tune; otherwise, tuning students' instruments for the sake of time may become a hindrance in the student's comprehensive music education.

Section leader

As a section leader in a larger ensemble, there are several responsibilities that must be met to strengthen the musical excellence and unity of the performing group. The section leader, or principal of a section, should be thoroughly prepared with his or her own musical part, since this will be the framework for the rest of the section. The section leader should also be ready to give advice in terms of style, articulation, phrasing, bowing, fingering, and other musical details. The section leader should also be proficient at keeping accurate tuning and should help to ensure the proper intonation of the entire section. The section leader is also responsible for interpreting any directives the conductor may give concerning musical interpretation such as dynamics, phrasing, articulation, and character.

Acoustical considerations for instrumental ensemble arrangement

When creating an arrangement for instrumental ensemble formations, there are several key acoustical considerations for the given ensemble to execute the optimal performance. A general guideline holds that softer instruments with important melody lines should sit near the front so that the audience can easily hear their sound. The seating arrangement of the ensemble should be so that when accompanying parts play softer to balance with the projecting melody, those instruments will not pull back so softly as a deficiency, but will still be able to support the melody line expressively and imaginatively. Thus, instrument groups with similar lines should be seated together as well as instrument groups with counter-melodies. This allows the musicians to be more aurally aware of the ensemble and to play with more confidence and freedom.

Jazz standards

For a beginning jazz band, a director should choose repertoire based on the opportunity it presents to play and experiment in the new idiom, taking advantage of the unique aspects of jazz music in a way that is educational and engaging. These features may include focusing on swing feeling, sectional solos, and other harmonic and structural features. Charts should provide the opportunity for students to take improvised solos, and students on all instruments, including the rhythm section, should be encouraged to experiment with improvisation. Popular publishers with charts for beginning jazz bands include Hal Leonard, Alfred, and Kendor. These arrangements are tailored to beginning musicians and may include sample solos that can be used as teaching tools. The director may wish to consider jazz standards with common chord changes such as "I've Got Rhythm" or a simple 12-bar blues. Over the course of the school year, the director may want to find charts that will allow different soloists to play featured parts.

Once the basics of improvisation have been established, the next step is to apply that learning in the context of a full song. This song will likely follow the standard head/solos/head structure. Full tunes for the beginning improviser should have characteristics that allow a student to focus her attention on a limited number of variables at one time. Songs should have a moderate tempo, a strong tonal center, and preferably no more than three or four different chords. These characteristics will allow the student time to play within each chord, focus on only the notes that are "strong" within the different chords of the song, and appreciate the sound of the same notes in different chordal contexts. The goal in introducing improvisation within this context is to reduce the number of choices of what note to play, a common hurdle for the beginning improviser, and direct the student's focus to playing with confidence, remaining oriented within the song while improvising, and other aspects of performance – rhythm, dynamics, space that eventually lead to more varied and interesting improvisations.

Fostering a relaxed instrumental playing approach

Approaching instrumental playing in a healthy manner requires a relaxed body to prevent injuries and to enhance instrumental tone and resonance. Physical tension in a musician can translate into an unpleasant, thinner, and pinched sound. Music educators can foster a relaxed approach to instrumental playing through daily instructional activities that encourage flexibility and freedom at the instrument. Rehearsals and music classes that start with physical stretching help students to release any existing tension, while signaling to the body a time for increased blood flow and loose joints. Music educators can implement warm-ups that involve tensing and releasing the shoulders so students can feel the presence and absence of tension in their bodies. Consistent and frequent reminders for a student to relax any tension will also help to make a relaxed approach a habit for the student.

Concert length and pacing

A concert planned for a beginning middle school band will differ widely from a concert planned for an advanced high school concert band. The beginning middle school band will have had little experience with performances and may still be working through rudimentary techniques and skills on their instruments. Repertoire for the beginning middle school band will focus mostly on easily accessible beginner works. The advanced high school concert band, however, will have at least a few years of experience performing and playing their instruments. Repertoire selection for the advanced concert band will have a wider range of intermediate to advanced works. Endurance is also an issue for the beginning band; concert length will be shorter, with shorter musical works and more frequent changes. The advanced high school band will be able to perform longer works of music with less frequent breaks.

Hand-horn technique for French horn

Hand-horn technique, also known as right-hand technique, is the placing of the right hand inside the bell of the horn. The technique was derived from early versions of the instrument, which had no valves. In these instruments, notes between the open partials of the harmonic series were played by opening and closing the throat of the bell with the hand. When valves were added, horn players still played with the right hand inside the bell in order to produce a slightly darker tone, more easily control pitch, and perform extended techniques such as stopped horn and echo horn. There are two methods for hand placement inside the bell. In the American method, the hand is held flat with the metal touching the back of the hand, with some of the horn's weight supported by the thumb. In the French method, the right hand is held out flat with palm down and the thumb forming a 90-degree angle with the hand, and some of the horn's weight is supported by the first knuckles and the back of the hand.

Trumpet and trombone

The trumpet and trombone share all the most popular mutes, with a trumpet and trombone version of each of the straight mute, cup mute, bucket mute, wah-wah mute, plunger, and hat. The difference between a trumpet mute and one for trombone is principally one of scale. The straight mute results in a tinny, metallic sound. The cup mute produces a muffled, darker tone and was common in trumpet sections during the classic big band era of the 1930s and 1940s. The bucket mute produces a softer tone and reduces the piercing quality of loud or high notes that can be amplified by other mutes. The wah-wah mute, often known by the brand-name Harmon mute, produces a buzzed tone, and for trumpet is often associated with Miles Davis during his cool jazz period. The plunger and the hat mute are used similarly, with the musician playing with one hand while manipulating the mute over the front of the bell with the other.

Multiple mallet techniques used by marimba players

Good mallet technique for marimba players allows the musicians a free range of color and technical possibilities, and starts with one mallet in each hand. Once the two-mallet grip has been learned with a flexible grip, the student usually learns the four-mallet grip next. The three main multiple mallet grips are the traditional crossed grip, the Burton grip, and the Musser/Stevens grip. The traditional grip places the second mallet between the index and middle fingers while grasping the end of the second mallet with the ring finger and pinky. The traditional grip has a higher rate of tension and less support than the other grips. The Burton grip places the second mallet between the index and middle fingers and the end of the mallet underneath all four fingers. The Musser/Stevens grip places the first mallet between the thumb and index fingers, and the second mallet between the middle and ring fingers so that the mallets are not crossed. The Musser/Stevens provides the most independence of mallet movement.

Body, arm, and finger position on the drumstick for proper snare drum technique

To execute proper snare drum technique, full attention must be made to develop the body, arm, and finger position of the player. The body should be in a fully relaxed and comfortable position without allowing the back to slouch or lean in. A seated body position in playing the snare drum should allow the feet to be flat on the floor with the legs spread evenly. The drum set should always be positioned to the player so that the player does not have to adjust unnaturally to the set. The player should be seated facing directly in front of the snare drum and not to the side or from below. The arms should always be relaxed and should hang at the body's side without unnecessary tension. The snare player should grip the drumstick firmly and in a relaxed manner so that each stroke has a flowing yet controlled movement with a full, legato sound.

Instructional Emphasis: Choral and Instrumental

Dynamic markings

The dynamic markings commonly used in music come from the written Italian musical tradition of the seventeenth century. The following markings are in order of increasing loudness. Pianissimo, abbreviated pp, indicates that the player should play very soft. Piano, abbreviated p, indicates that the player should play soft. Mezzo piano, abbreviated mp, indicates that the player should play moderately soft. Mezzo forte, abbreviated mf, indicates that the player should play moderately loud. Forte, abbreviated f, indicates that the player should play loud. Fortissimo, abbreviated ff, indicates that the play should play very loud. Dynamic markings that indicate a gradual change include crescendo and decrescendo or diminuendo. A crescendo indicates that the player should play increasingly louder. A decrescendo or diminuendo indicates that the player should play increasingly softer.

Warming up

Warming up serves several important physical and mental functions for the group ensemble. Mentally, it has the effect of centering and adjusting the ensemble to an appropriate mental state for performance and establishing proper physiological cues for posture, breathing, etc. Warm-ups serve as a unifying tool for all members of the ensemble to begin listening to each other as a musical entity and adjusting sound according to the group. Physically, the warm-up promotes blood flow to the entire body, making every member ready to respond to the physical demands of making music. Though easy to overlook, the warm-up serves an important function for the instrument as well as the body. Whether a brass, woodwind, string, percussion, or vocal instrument, every instrument should be properly warmed and its mechanisms stretched and lubricated. Without a proper warm-up, singers could damage their vocal mechanisms, and the tonal quality of instrumentalists could suffer.

Intonation spot checks

During a rehearsal, the director should use various techniques to ensure the accurate intonation of the ensemble. Aside from beginning each rehearsal with accurate tuning, the director can use spot checks of each different section as teaching moments as well. Isolating the instrument or vocal groups for intonation spot checks teaches the students to listen attentively to themselves and also to the surrounding students. Students will have opportunities to practice the appropriate procedures of adjusting pitch on their respective instruments. Brass instruments with slides can adjust their pitches through their slides; woodwinds can adjust their pitches through adjustments of the mouthpieces; string instruments can adjust their pitches through tuning pegs; vocalists can adjust their pitches through minor adjustments of their vocal mechanisms. When participating in intonation spot checks, students will learn to produce a consistent pitch with their breath or their open strings.

Program notes

Program notes should serve as a helpful guide for the audience while listening to a musical performance. It should provide key elements to understanding the work, such as contextual background, historical context, first performance, scoring, musical style, and possible details to listen for. The writer should avoid personal anecdotes, footnotes, irrelevant facts and details, musical examples or excerpts, exclusively technical terminology, or effusive emotional descriptions. Program notes should be insightful and engaging, and should further the enjoyment of the listening audience. The program notes should be thoroughly researched, geared toward the level of understanding of the audience, whether for a young audience or for expert theorists. If possible, the writer should include unique and engaging facts such as the initial reception through a first review or the dedication of the work.

Preparation for program notes involves extensive and thorough research on the musical work as well as its historical context and contextual background. When first starting to research, it is important to consult a variety of sources for the most accurate information. A good starting point for any music research is the *New Grove Dictionary of Music and Musicians*. As a standard, authoritative text, this source offers the most up-to-date and complete resource available. After consulting the *New Grove Dictionary*, it is useful to use composer biographies, orchestral music resources, CD liner notes, primary notes on the score, and other published collections of program notes. The writer should also check the text and translations for the most accurate rendering. Once researched, the program notes should be written, including historical, biographical, and contextual information as well as information about the work itself.

Concert etiquette

As a leader of a student's music education, the music educator should be an advocate of proper concert etiquette. Although there are many aspects of music for a student to learn, it is equally important for a student to understand the proper way to act both as a concert musician as well as an audience member. As such, concert etiquette should be an integral part of every rehearsal and lesson. The student can begin practicing such performance etiquette as proper sitting or standing posture, as well as appropriate eye contact. The student can also begin to practice such things as bowing after performance as well as entrance etiquette. The students in the classroom can practice good audience technique through peer performance, exhibiting polite listening manners, withholding clapping between movements, and applause after a performance. The music educator can also take the opportunity during parent conferences or before a concert to address members of the audience regarding proper concert etiquette.

Publicizing music programs and events

In a music program, there is usually a limited budget for yearly expenses; music educators can stretch the program budget by implementing cost-effective methods of publicizing music programs and events. One area in which the music educator can minimize cost is through concert publications. Instead of using costly printed posters, the music educator can take advantage of social media, publicizing upcoming events through the Internet instead of through paper. If the program still needs paper publications, the music educator can use smaller flyers that will cost less than larger posters. The music educator can also publicize music programs through the help of a parent committee; working as a team, supporters of the music program can publicize upcoming concerts and events through fundraising efforts while also spreading information about the program. The music educator can also eliminate the cost of program notes by having an announcer give brief introductory information between musical works.

Performance venues

Any audience member should be aware of the performance venue for a concert, as there are different etiquettes for different performance venues. In a classical concert, the audience usually does not talk during a performance as it is considered disruptive, and applause is only polite at the end of a musical work. In contrast, jazz audiences can clap or give sound approval at any point of the performance to exhibit admiration for an improvised section or solo. At a rock concert, not only can the audience clap or give sound approval at any time, audience members can freely talk throughout the concert. Although the appropriate sound levels of the various audiences differ, some things remain constant at any venue.

Audiences should arrive early to settle into the venue and feel comfortable. Audience members should always be aware of photography and videography regulations. Also, audiences should always be responsible for their children at a concert.

Sound production

For sound to be produced, there must be a vibration, or pressure oscillation through a medium that is transmitted through the air, through the mechanical structure of the ear to be perceived as sound in the brain. The source of the oscillation can be any simple resonator, which as it moves through space creates fluctuations in the pressure of the surrounding air. The string of a violin, the membrane of a percussion instrument, and the reed of a woodwind instrument all act as resonators. Energy imparted to them through the motion of a bow, the strike of a drumstick, or wind blown across the reed act to set the oscillations in motion. The subsequent physical vibration of the surrounding air travels as complex sound waves outwards. As these sound waves travel towards the listener, the membrane of the human eardrum perceives the sound waves and converts the frequencies into aural perception where the listener will hear either a tone or noise.

Pure tone vs. tone produced by an instrument

In acoustics, a pure tone is defined as a simple sine wave whose frequency stays constant over time. Frequency, measured in Hertz as the number of cycles over time, is perceived by the human ear as pitch. A tone produced by an instrument, however, is not a simple sine wave but is in fact a complex wave; no musical instrument produces a pure tone. When an instrument plays a sound, there is a primary resonating frequency called the fundamental frequency, joined by harmonics and overtones as well. The harmonic frequencies resonate at integer multiples of the fundamental, and change the overall waveform into a composite waveform. Pure tones contain no harmonics or overtones. The various timbres of the different instruments are greatly dependent on the waveform profile of the complex wave.

Reverberation time

Reverberation time is considered to be the time it takes for sound to decay, usually by 60 decibels from its direct signal. When the direct signal interacts with the materials of a space, some of the energy is absorbed by objects in the space or by absorbent wall materials, while the rest is reflected. As the sound waves bounce off of the various surfaces multiple times, the resultant sound waves are collectively known as reverberation; the energy of the sound waves decays over time until there is little energy left to travel. Many factors affect reverberation time, including size of the space, materials within the space, ceiling height, shape of the space, and the amount of people within the space. The longest reverberation times tend to be those of cathedrals and large concert halls, while the shortest reverberation times would be those of open fields or soundproof rehearsal rooms. A football field would have little reverberation time, as the direct signal would already be weakened in the long distances it takes to reach the bleachers as well as the lack of a ceiling to reflect the sound waves. A rehearsal room would have slightly more reverberation time, given the presence of a ceiling; the reverberation time of rehearsal rooms vary considerably depending on the wall materials. A concert hall would have significantly more reverberation time than a rehearsal room, as the design of the space usually increases the blend of sound and thus reverberation. A cathedral would have the most reverberation time of the list, with highly reflective walls typical of cathedrals and the intricate ceilings in which sound waves would have multiples points to reflect and travel.

Reflected sound and direct sound

In an environment other than the theoretical free field where there are no physical objects for sound waves to react to, sound waves undergo reflection, diffraction, and refraction in a performance space. As sound waves leave the source, the energy of the air radiates spherically from the source. This direct sound continues to move outwards until it hits a physical surface. Depending on the absorbency of the physical surface, the sound is either absorbed into heat by an absorbent surface, thereby lessening the intensity of the sound, or it is reflected by a hard surface, thereby redirecting the direction of the radiating sound waves. As sound waves reflect back towards the source, they create the acoustical phenomenon of reverberation, as the listener continues to hear the direct sound followed closely by the reflected sound.

Frequency and perceived pitch

Frequency refers to the number of oscillations of a waveform per second, also known as Hertz. Pitch is the human perception of the fundamental frequency of a sound wave, and can be affected by distance from the source, amplitude, physiology, and mental expectation. The average human listener can hear frequencies between 16 Hz and ~20,000 Hz. In music, relevant frequencies range from 20 Hz to 5,000 Hz. The range of a guitar, for instance, is 82 Hz of the lowest E to 330 Hz of the highest E. For the most part, humans hear higher frequencies of oscillations as higher pitches, and lower frequencies of oscillations as lower pitches. Over time, certain frequencies have been standardized for a particular pitch. Concert a', for example, has been measured at 440 Hz since the twentieth century.

Variations in amplitude

For every sound wave, there are two basic aspects to consider: frequency and amplitude. Frequency refers to the number of sound waves per second, also known as Hertz, and is perceived by the human ear as a musical pitch. Amplitude refers to the height of the sound wave and is measured in decibels. Variations in amplitude are generally perceived by the human ear as changes in loudness; the higher the decibel level, the louder the sound. Variations in amplitude can also be perceived in an attack of a tone. A plucked tone has a sharp attack, and the waveform reaches its peak amplitude quickly, while the amplitude gradually decreases as the sound fades away. Variations in amplitude can also be found in tremolos and vibratos. Although vibratos are generally known as frequency modulation (FM), and tremolos are generally known as amplitude modulation (AM), in execution, both forms of modulation are usually present.

Partials

The concept of partials refers to the specific acoustic property of audible tones. The most basic tone, a pure sine wave, has a frequency f that determines the pitch of the wave. In musical sound, however, sound waves are usually much more complex than that of a pure tone, and consist of several different frequencies that become superimposed into one complex sine wave that the human listener perceives as a single tone. The different frequencies of the complex wave are termed partials and change the displacement of the combined frequencies. The partial frequencies give the different instruments their unique timbres, as the different components of the sound produced by an oboe, guitar, marimba, glockenspiel, or cymbal superimpose to a unique complex wave configuration of pressure over time.

Overtones

The concept of overtones refers to a specific acoustic property of sound. For every one frequency, there are multiple other frequencies that vibrate through the resonant space through its normal modes. Every instrument has a distinct set of normal modes that vibrate through certain frequencies, giving its timbre and tone. The lowest sounding frequency is termed the fundamental frequency; all other frequencies above the fundamental are termed overtones. Overtones are partial frequencies and can be harmonic or non-harmonic. Harmonic overtones are those that are integral multiples of the fundamental. Non-harmonic overtones are those that are not integral multiples of the fundamental. Most musical instruments have overtone frequencies that are near to their harmonic frequencies. Instruments such as brass instruments, gongs, cymbals, and timpanis have overtone frequencies that are more distinct from their harmonic frequencies.

Harmonics

The concept of harmonics refers to a specific acoustic property of sound. For every one frequency called the fundamental frequency, there exists a series of other frequencies called the harmonic set that are integral multiples of the fundamental: $f1$, $f2$, $f3$, etc. For every fundamental frequency, f, the frequency of the nth harmonic is equal to f times n. The harmonic frequencies have acoustically pure tones and most approximate the pitches in standard Western music tuning: the first harmonic occurs an octave above the fundamental; the second harmonic occurs an additional fifth above; the third harmonic occurs an additional fourth above; the fourth occurs an additional third above; etc. The harmonic series helps to define the human perception of pitch; it is so integral, in fact, that humans still perceive the fundamental pitch of the harmonic series even when the fundamental frequency is missing.

Performance competencies

Students in Pre-K should experience music as much as possible through listening, feeling, moving, and experimenting with their own vocal pitch and timbre. Children in this age range should be encouraged to freely use their voices in singing, chanting, and speaking along with music accompaniment and on their own. Students in Pre-K should experience a wide range of instrumental sounds and improvise their own melodies and patterns on different instruments. Students should practice relating musical sounds to other objects, symbols, and animals that are familiar to them, to engage their imagination and encourage creative responses. Students in Pre-K should become increasingly accurate in their pitch matching and rhythm matching through their voices or on instruments. Students should experience a wide variety of genres and styles as well as be able to identify basic differences and changes in music.

Appropriately leveled, culturally diverse music selections

As a music educator, it is important to select appropriately leveled, culturally diverse music selections to reflect the musical diversity within the global community as well as to challenge the students in a variety of styles and genres. Music directors should select a variety of music that is below, at, and above an ensemble's level to provide opportunities for in-depth expressive growth without technical obstacles, as well as music that challenges the students technically to reach the next level. Music directors can consult state contest repertoire lists for a general list of appropriate repertoire, as well as published repertoire books. Culturally diverse composers such as Soon Hee Newbold, William Grant Still, Dorothy Rudd Moore, and Yasuhide Ito offer many works that would be appropriate for an advanced high school ensemble.

Core repertoire list

When devising a core repertoire list for an ensemble, it is important to take many musical aspects into consideration. A core repertoire list should provide a strong framework of music education for the students, factoring in the students' musical growth and development. A core repertoire list should include a variety of rhythmic features that challenge the ensemble's technical abilities. The harmonic language of the repertoire list should be varied and in a wide range of genres. The melodic lines within the repertoire should exhibit creative writing and expressive interest for the students. The repertoire should also be well orchestrated, providing musical interest in all sections of the ensemble, as well as providing a balance between tutti and thinner textures. The repertoire should provide some works that are deeply expressive, to allow students to expand their musical expressive language. The core repertoire list should be well sequenced in introducing new musical concepts as well reinforcing old ones.

Colleagues, mentors, conferences, and publishers

A conscientious director should be willing to look to a diverse variety of sources for repertoire. By drawing from colleagues, mentors, conferences, and publishers, the director can tap the experience of people of different tastes, ages, backgrounds, and musical circles. The suggestions of those with a different approach to choosing repertoire can be particularly valuable, as these suggestions are the most likely to be overlooked by a search undertaken independently. Publishers may be useful due to their access not only to their own catalogs, including back catalog that may have been previously overlooked, but also to the catalogs in the publisher's extended network. As publishing houses have consolidated and collections have become digitized, repertoire that may have only been available from small boutique publishers has become available for wider circulation.

Rhythmic accuracy

Many times, rhythmic inaccuracy in beginner students results from a lack of basic reinforcement of the concept of a steady beat. Beginner music students will benefit from heavy reinforcement of a steady beat through movement activities such as dancing to the beat of a song, clapping or tapping along to a rhyme, swaying back and forth while counting out loud, or other forms of multi-sensory learning that involve the kinesthetic mode as well as the aural mode. Beginner music students will also benefit from visual and aural modeling from the music educator as well as from peers. Peer learning can be a great source of motivation and encouragement to learn, as students will generally want to match the level of their peers. Music educators should also introduce the concept of the heartbeat in practicing a steady beat, relating the abstract concept of tempo and meter to a familiar one of the body.

Pitch reading

Pitch reading can be a challenging concept for beginner students, as many mental processes occur from the written visual cue to the symbolic processing, to knowledge retrieval, to the answering output. For beginner students, it is important to have a reference when pitch reading, whether it is middle C or another referential pitch. Students should also understand the spatial relationships required in note reading, that higher on the staff also means higher in pitch and that lower on the staff also means lower in pitch. The music educator should ensure that the beginner student understands how to play high and low on his or her respective instrument before continuing the lessons into more complex playing. Similarly to language learning, the music educator should also provide ample reinforcement and practice in pitch reading as the student begins to integrate the musical symbols with aural and pitch meaning.

Rote learning vs. intervallic note reading

The rote method of note reading refers to teaching a student to read notes from memory. Techniques to teach students to read by rote include mnemonic devices such as the lines of the treble clef ("Every Good Boy Does Fine"), the spaces of the treble clef ("FACE"), the lines of the bass clef ("Good Boys Do Fine Always"), and the spaces of the bass clef ("All Cows Eat Grass"). Intervallic note reading refers to the method of reading by intervallic relationships, i.e., a third up, a second down, a fourth up, etc. Intervallic

- 78 -

note reading relies on spatial visualization, while rote reading relies on memorization. While both methods of note reading result in proficient musical skills, pros and cons exist for each. In rote reading, students are more quickly able to identify note names; however, sight-reading may be slightly slower because of the added mental processing of labels. In intervallic reading, students are more quickly able to identify direction and intervals during sight-reading; however, note naming may be slightly more difficult as students must first process intervals.

Pyramid model of balance and blend

The pyramid model of balance and blend refers to the theory that higher-pitched singers and instruments should play softer than the lowest-pitched singers and instruments, so that an ideal balance exists between the treble and the bass. In this model, the-higher pitched section will also be able to hear the bass for better intonation and blend. In the pyramid model, the bass voices and instruments constitute the bottom rung of the pyramid; the width of the pyramid determines the overall volume of the ensemble. As the pyramid rises, higher-pitched voices and instruments are stacked above the bass section to the tip of the pyramid where the highest treble section is placed. The higher the voice or instrument is on the pyramid, the softer the sound should be. To apply it to an ensemble, the director should have the bass section play or sing a fortissimo, the tenor section a forte, the alto section a mezzo-forte, and the soprano section, a mezzo-piano, so that the full ensemble can experience the balance and blend of the pyramid model.

Ensemble rehearsal strategies

During an ensemble rehearsal, there are many rehearsal strategies to take on technically challenging passages. The music director should first determine if the technically challenging passage is the result of a lack of individual practice. If so, the director should show the students in detail the correct way to practice individually and at home. If the passage still presents technical challenges for the ensemble, the music director should take the ensemble through the passage slowly and rhythmically to identify the probable origin of the difficulty. Then the educator will be able to assist the ensemble in note accuracy, technical facility, and fluency in playing. Once the ensemble has the tools to fix the challenging passage, the ensemble should go through the passage again slowly in isolation and then slowly speed up the challenging passage until performance tempo has been reached. The ensemble should practice scales, arpeggios, and technical etudes to further develop technical skills.

Diversity of repertoire

Diversity of repertoire is an important and current topic for music directors in the present era of concert programming. Good concert programming will reflect the diversity that the audience experiences in the world around them. Concerts must engage the audience with relevant and fresh perspectives through culturally diverse and new works as well as through the musical standards of the past. Showcasing contemporary new works alongside a traditional classical work can inform and rejuvenate the audience's listening ear. Programming new works along with old works also illuminates the performance practices of the past, where Beethoven and Wagner were featuring works of the present along with the past. Students will have a broader musical perspective by experiencing music from different cultures, genres, and time periods. Widely diverse concert programs can unite audience members of the past, of today, and of the future.

Practice Test

Practice Questions

1. Which of the following notes makes a C major chord triad?
   a. C, E, and G
   b. C, E♭, and G
   c. C, E, G, and B
   d. C, E♭, G, and B♭

2. There is a note between every natural note on a scale except
   a. C and D, and G and A
   b. B and C, and E and F
   c. B and C, and D and E
   d. A and B, and E and F

3. A musician playing a B♭ clarinet sees the written note c. How will that note actually sound?
   a. C
   b. B♭
   c. A
   d. C♯

4. In the first inversion for the chord C major, which note is transposed up an octave?
   a. C
   b. E
   c. G
   d. E♭

5. In standard twelve-bar blues form, where would one expect to find the "turnaround"?
   a. the first bar
   b. the fourth bar
   c. the eighth bar
   d. the twelfth bar

6. What is the difference between 3/4 time and 6/8 time, by definition?
   a. There is no difference.
   b. 3/4 time uses three beats per measure, while 6/8 time uses six beats per measure.
   c. In 3/4 time the quarter note acts as the one beat unit, while in 6/8 time the eighth note acts as the one beat unit.
   d. 3/4 time uses a quicker tempo.

7. Which of the following tempos is played between 120 and 168 beats per minute?
   a. Presto
   b. Moderato
   c. Allegro
   d. Largo

- 80 -

8. Which of the following is an example of *leitmotif*?

    a. The distinctive, repetitive change from E to F in John Williams' theme for Jaws
    b. Pieces in which an orchestra accompanies a harpsichord, as composed by Bach
    c. The challenging key changes in César Franck's Symphony in D minor
    d. The book containing the words to Giuseppe Verdi's *La Traviata*

9. The following musical staff represents which key signature?

    a. D major
    b. A major
    c. G major
    d. C major

Use the musical excerpt below for questions 10-12:

10. The tempo of the preceding piece by Frédéric Chopin could best be described by which of the following statements?
    a. Slower than largo but faster than largamente
    b. Faster than andante but slower than moderato
    c. Slower than andante but faster than adagietto
    d. About 60 beats per minute

11. This piece represents which style of folk dance?
    a. polka
    b. mazurka
    c. an dro
    d. kolo

- 81 -

12. Which of the following performance styles are denoted musically by thin, curved lines over most of the notes?
    a. legato
    b. staccato
    c. fortissimo
    d. mezzo piano

13. Intervals larger than an octave are:
    a. octave intervals
    b. compound intervals
    c. perfect fifths
    d. intervals larger than an octave do not exist

14. Diminished chords are considered dissonant for which of the following reasons:
    a. They sound "sad."
    b. They lack a tonal center.
    c. They are barely audible.
    d. They are viewed with universal disdain and absent from most popular recordings.

Use the musical excerpt below for questions 15-16:

15. Which of the following well-known classical music compositions features the preceding musical passage?
    a. "The Blue Danube"
    b. "Brandenburg Concerto, No. 5"
    c. "Pictures at an Exhibition"
    d. "Claire de Lune"

16. What is the key signature of the preceding piece?
    a. B-flat major
    b. C-sharp major
    c. A-flat minor
    d. C major

17. The bass line in Michael Jackson's "Billy Jean," the three-note bass line in the Temptations' "Papa Was a Rollin' Stone," and the "take a chance, take a chance" chant in the ABBA tune "Take a Chance on Me" are all examples of:
    a. solfège
    b. ostinato
    c. tessitura
    d. pizzicato

18. What is the relative difference in frequency between these two notes?

   a. 1:1
   b. 2:1
   c. 4:1
   d. 8:1

Use the musical passage below for questions 19-22:

19. The preceding musical passage is written in which time signature?
    a. 2/2 time
    b. 3/4 time
    c. 4/4 time
    d. 5/4 time

20. The preceding musical passage can be described best as a:
   a. chorale
   b. fugue
   c. gigue
   d. cantata

21. The "tr" written above the staff in measure seven indicates that the performer should:
   a. trill
   b. tie the notes together for the rest of the measure
   c. tenuto
   d. turn

22. There are no alto notes until the sixth measure. When they do appear, the alto notes form the:
   a. coda
   b. middle entry
   c. subject
   d. countersubject

23. Which of the following composers is most strongly associated with the Romantic Period?
   a. Johann Sebastian Bach
   b. Maurice Ravel
   c. Aaron Copeland
   d. Johannes Brahms

24. What was the goal of The Five—Mily Balakirev, César Cui, Modest Mussorgsky, Nikolai Rimsky-Korsakov, and Alexander Borodin—the group of composers who met periodically in Saint Petersburg, Russia, between 1856 and 1870?
   a. To study other styles of music, specifically those in Western Europe, so that Russian music might properly develop and be taken seriously by composers and   audiences there
   b. To create a style of art music that was uniquely and characteristically Russian
   c. To bring music education to the poor people living in underdeveloped areas
   d. To use music as a way of challenging the rule of the Tsars

25. What style of music traditionally is played by a sextet—a group consisting of two violins, a piano, a double bass, and two bandoneóns?
   a. Tango
   b. Salsa
   c. Flamenco
   d. Tejano

26. Bebop was a dramatic shift from the traditional jazz of the middle 20th century because it
   a. was performed by integrated groups of musicians
   b. employed a strict 4/4 time signature
   c. deemphasized the role of the trumpet and other brass instruments
   d. used asymmetrical phrasing and an expanded role for the rhythm section

27. The folk music of which of the following cultures or countries is primarily percussive in nature?
    a. Finnish
    b. Peruvian
    c. Mongolian
    d. Ewe

28. Other than early drums formed from hitting logs with a blunt tool, the precursors to which of the following musical instruments generally are considered the oldest?
    a. trumpets
    b. violins
    c. flutes
    d. xylophones

29. The Hammond organ originally was used by
    a. U.S. churches in the 1930s
    b. blues, rock, and jazz musicians in the 1960s
    c. Baroque composers in the 1640s
    d. English composers in the 1890s

30. Which of the following types of music is *not* constructed monophonically?
    a. Gregorian chants
    b. Indian classical music
    c. a Bach fugue
    d. most troubadour songs

31. Which of the following keyboard instruments that evolved in late Medieval times produces sound from a series of strings that is plucked?
    a. clavichord
    b. harpsichord
    c. piano
    d. hurdy gurdy

32. Which composer wrote the famous guitar concerto *Concerto de Aranjuez* in 1939?
    a. Fernando Sor
    b. Manuel Barrueco
    c. Joaquín Rodrigo
    d. Francisco Tárrega

33. *Kan ha diskan*, the most widely known music of Brittany, is characterized by which musical form?
    a. call and response
    b. chamber music
    c. microtonal music
    d. percussion only

34. In which of the following musicals would one expect to hear klezmer music?
    a. Fiddler on the Roof
    b. The Sound of Music
    c. Oklahoma!
    d. A Chorus Line

35. Which of the following composers was known best for creating operettas?
    a. Wolfgang Amadeus Mozart
    b. Giacomo Puccini
    c. Sir Arthur Sullivan
    d. Giuseppe Verdi

36. Which of the following is generally considered the first widely popular hip hop single in the United States?
    a. "Walk This Way" by Run-d.M.c. and Aerosmith
    b. "Rapper's Delight" by The Sugarhill Gang
    c. "Hit 'Em Up" by Tupac Shakur
    d. "Don't Believe the Hype" by Public Enemy

37. *Castrati* were employed to sing in choirs because which of the following groups was banned from performing in churches?
    a. Protestants
    b. women
    c. commoners
    d. boys

38. Which of the following musical genres was *one* of the influences in the development of Tejano music?
    a. Incan music
    b. African music
    c. Peruvian music
    d. German music

39. The MP3 format allows a CD track to be stored at a fraction of its original size because the process
    a. copies the original file at a lower sound volume
    b. removes selected vocal or instrument tracks
    c. removes selected information, including frequencies that are too high or too low for humans to hear
    d. converts the digital information to analog information

40. Music of the Renaissance began relying on what interval as a consonance, which previously had been regarded as dissonant?
    a. second
    b. third
    c. fifth
    d. None of these, because intervals were not used until the Baroque period.

41. Which of the following instruments would be integral to Indonesian *gamelan*?
    a. bulbul tarang
    b. qinqin
    c. gong
    d. kora

- 87 -

42. Bedřich Smetana's "Vltava," also named "The Moldau," is a piece of music that describes
    a. the Russian victory over invading French armies in 1812
    b. an adventurer's attempt to escape an evil king's trolls
    c. the course of a river as it winds through Central Europe
    d. an audio tour of an orchestra, intended to encourage a young person's interest in classical music

43. Which of the following pairs of composers lived and worked during the same time period?
    a. Antonio Vivaldi and Friedrich Chopin
    b. Gustav Holst and Johann Sebastian Bach
    c. Johann Pachelbel and Franz Liszt
    d. Pyotr Ilyich Tchaikovsky and Edvard Grieg

44. Of the commonly accepted and understood time periods into which Western classical music has been divided, which period is associated most strongly with musical nationalism?
    a. Baroque
    b. Classical
    c. Romantic
    d. Contemporary

45. Which of the following describes the best method for determining the proper-sized violin for a student musician?
    a. Choosing a violin that is about a quarter as long as the student is tall
    b. Allowing the student to choose an instrument based on what "feels right"
    c. Choosing a violin whose scroll extends just to the base of the student's hand
    d. Choosing a violin that allows the student's fingers to curl comfortably around the scroll and allows the elbows to bend slightly

46. Which are the best tuning pitches before a rehearsal or performance?
    a. Concert C # and Concert A, with exception of French horns
    b. Concert D and Concert B ♭, with the exception of flutes
    c. Concert B ♭ and Concert F, with the exception of saxophones
    d. Concert F and Concert A ♭, with the exception of clarinets

47. A music teacher found guilty of willful copyright infringement for personal financial gain faces maximum penalties of which of the following?
    a. a warning from the company he or she has wronged and a complaint to his or her state's licensing board
    b. two years' probation
    c. unspecified statutory damages ranging from $750 to $30,000
    d. criminal fines up to $250,000 and/or a five year jail sentence

48. A band director wants to record a student performance of a copyrighted work for educational or archival purposes. How many copies can the director make without paying a fee?
    a. as many copies as he or she wants, as long as the purpose is educational
    b. one copy
    c. two copies, one for him or herself and one for the student
    d. no more than ten copies

49. A choir director believes an arrangement of "People" would be perfect for her concert choir, except for one part near the end that she deems too difficult for her tenors. Can she modify the arrangement to make it easier to sing, provided she has obeyed all other copyright law?
    a. Yes, as long as she retains the fundamental character of the piece and does not alter or add lyrics.
    b. Yes, because paying the licensing fee permits gives her wide artistic latitude to arrange.
    c. No, because the licensing fee covers only that particular arrangement.
    d. Yes, because several appeals courts have wrangled over this kind of issue for decades and have not come to a clear conclusion.

50. A music history teacher desires to construct a lesson based upon the eccentric brilliance of keyboard master Glenn Gould. As part of the lesson, he would like to play a copyrighted CD recording of Gould's harpsichord work. If he wanted to follow copyright law, the teacher would have to do which of the following?
    a. Obtain permission from ASCAP, BMI, or another licensing group.
    b. Pay a modest fee, equal to face value of the CD's purchase price.
    c. Do nothing, since his role as a teacher allows this type of presentation.
    d. Recorded performances, even for classes, are not permitted under U.S. copyright law.

51. Which of the following techniques can help the beginning clarinetist "cross the break"?
    a. have him/her play in the low register and then activate the register key
    b. encourage her to blow with more force
    c. require her to play it scale-wise
    d. rely less on the throat registers

52. What is the proper use of the finger ring for trumpet players?
    a. the place where the little finger should rest during performance
    b. the place where the ring finger should rest during performances
    c. It should be used only for keeping the horn steady while turning pages or inserting a mute.
    d. Modern trumpets are not manufactured with a finger ring.

53. What is the normal compass of a timpani?
    a. a minor third
    b. a perfect fourth
    c. a perfect fifth
    d. a major seventh

54. How often should brass players oil the valves of their instruments in order to prevent sticking?
    a. once a day
    b. about once a week
    c. once a month
    d. only when the valves begin to stick

55. Which of the following would satisfy a young musical learner's *kinesthetic* needs?
    a. learning to read musical notation by listening to music
    b. hitting notes on a xylophone with the correct rhythm
    c. sitting and listening to a recording of "Peter and the Wolf"
    d. evaluating a peer's singing

56. Which of the following statements is true about the viola?
   a. It is tuned the same as a violin.
   b. It is a mainstay of the symphony but is rarely used in chamber music.
   c. It uses alto or "viola" clef, a clef that is otherwise rarely used.
   d. It is larger than the violin, but it uses a finer bow.

57. Although the pitch of "concert A" is accepted almost universally for tuning, musicians attempting to play Baroque instruments (or modern instruments in a more "authentic" style) will often tune to "Baroque pitch," which is an A at what frequency?
   a. 220 Hz
   b. 415 Hz
   c. 440 Hz
   d. 880 Hz

58. Which of the following statements is true of tablature, or "tabs," for guitar and other stringed instruments?
   a. The courts have ruled that online providers of tabs are legally distributing music, despite challenges from the music industry.
   b. It is an excellent way to teach mastery of an instrument to beginning musicians.
   c. It clearly indicates important information about a piece of music, including key signature and tempo.
   d. It indicates the fingering position of pieces, note for note, for stringed instruments.

59. Which portion of a daily class lesson would be the best for teaching concentrated, fundamental lessons in voice training?
   a. at the beginning of class
   b. between the periods designated for learning and rehearsing specific pieces
   c. at the end of class
   d. Such teaching is not appropriate, since instructional time is limited and the appropriate place for voice training would be private lessons

60. Which of the following statements is true of vocal changes in developing adolescents?
   a. It is largely a myth and can be kept in check by teaching proper technique.
   b. Girls' singing voices do not change, although boys' singing voices do change.
   c. Because their voices change in unpredictable ways, boys should stop singing during the middle school years and then resume in high school.
   d. Girls' singing voices change just as boys' voices do.

61. Which of the following statements is true of the oboe?
   a. Young students should always begin playing an easier woodwind instrument prior to transitioning to oboe.
   b. Typically, the oboe is held nearly 90 degrees from the body.
   c. It uses a double reed.
   d. It is assembled in three parts.

62. Which of the following statements is true of program notes typically given to audience members during a performance?
    a. They are optional, at best.
    b. They only should include the names of the pieces and the composers.
    c. They should include the lyrics of vocal pieces.
    d. They should include the arrangers of the pieces rather than merely the composers.

63. Which of the following describes incorrect sitting posture for students singing in a choir?
    a. Sitting toward the back of the seat, with the back just touching the backrest.
    b. Feet slightly apart.
    c. Hips, spine, and head in line.
    d. Chest lifted to enhance breathing.

64. Which of the following describes incorrect standing posture for students singing in a choir?
    a. Knees slightly relaxed.
    b. Body straight; hips, back, and head in line.
    c. Feet together.
    d. Chest lifted, shoulders back, and arms at the side, comfortably.

65. Which of the following statements is true regarding music teachers' expected level of proficiency on their students' instruments?
    a. It is not necessary to be proficient on any instrument in order to be a competent band director.
    b. It is customary for instrumental music teachers to be proficient only in the section where their instrument of choice is located; for example, a trumpeter should be expected only to have proficiency with brass instruments.
    c. Teachers should have at least a passing familiarity with all of the instruments in the bands they are teaching.
    d. Band directors should be proficient on every instrument their students are playing.

66. A flute player taps her feet in order to keep time to music during performances and rehearsals. A young band director is unsure of what to do about this, as she knows that proper
concert etiquette is important when performing for the public. What should she do with the flute player?
    a. The director should do nothing; the flutist is tapping her foot in order to keep time.
    b. Students should develop internal rhythm. Besides, foot tapping is distracting. It should stop immediately.
    c. The flute player should be encouraged to tap her toe inside her shoe; a little foot motion is fine.
    d. The flute player's foot tapping is distracting when done alone; therefore, the entire flute section should be encouraged to tap their feet.

67. Which of the following statements is true about a band or choir director's conducting style?
    a. A band or choir director's conducting style is mostly for show.
    b. He or she should practice conducting in front of a mirror along with taped or recorded music in order to make sure his or her conducting style is rhythmic and appropriate.
    c. Conducting styles should be forceful and dynamic, since they bring out the most in students. Furthermore, the audience's attendance is due in part to see the conductor's work.
    d. Conducting style can help an ensemble keep time, but it rarely influences dynamics, and style.

68. Which of the following statements is *not* true about a school's musical instrumental practice rooms?
    a. Practice rooms are relatively expensive to build and maintain.
    b. Practice rooms should include indirect lighting or lighting projected from the rear.
    c. Practice rooms should include an electronic tuner.
    d. Practice rooms are among the most frequently used rooms after classrooms.

69. Which of the following statements is true regarding the piccolo?
    a. Even skilled flutists cannot play the piccolo without relearning another instrument.
    b. The D-flat piccolo is today's standard instrument.
    c. The piccolo uses less air, but the musician must blow that air more rapidly.
    d. The piccolo has the same flexibility in pitch as the flute.

70. Which of the following characteristics do the baritone and the euphonium have in common?
    a. The music for both instruments requires beginning players to read treble and bass clef equally.
    b. Both instruments are pitched to B-flat.
    c. Most models of both instruments sold and used in the United States come with four valves.
    d. Both instruments have the same size mouthpiece and bore.

71. Which of the following statements is true of the tuba?
    a. The number of tuba players in a band is entirely up to the number of players who want to play it and the desires of the band director.
    b. A tuba is the perfect instrument for a player who doesn't have a good ear.
    c. The best tuba players are the largest students.
    d. The tuba is made only in one key, F.

72. Which of the following is true about the needs of middle school vs. high school percussion inventories, with regard to size and number of instruments?
    a. They are the same or close to it.
    b. Middle school percussionists need drums only and probably do not need other instruments such as xylophones.
    c. A middle school percussion ensemble needs about half the instruments of a high school section.
    d. Middle school percussionists need snare drums only, and can move to the other drums later.

73. What sizes of violins are available for student musicians?
    a. full size only
    b. full and ½ sizes only
    c. full, ¼, ½, and 1/8 sizes
    d. full, 1/32, 1/16, 1/8, ¼, ½, and 3/4 sizes

74. Which of the following is true of extrinsic motivation in a music classroom?
    a. There are no uses for extrinsic motivation; all motivation from student musicians should come from within.
    b. Should be limited to routine, well-earned behaviors.
    c. Should be given for solving complex tasks related to music.
    d. Extrinsic motivation is banned by most school districts.

75. Which of the following is generally not true of a march?
    a. It has a lively, "up-beat" accompaniment.
    b. It is written in 2/4 time.
    c. It should feature slowed-down tempos when playing piano dynamics.
    d. It has an independent bass line.

76. Which is true of the amount of practice a student instrumentalist or singer should do every day?
    a. From the beginning, student musicians should practice at least an hour a day.
    b. Student musicians should not be expected to practice at first, especially if they are younger. There will be plenty of time to practice once they have more mastery.
    c. Students should practice a half-hour or so each day, then ideally work up to more than an hour every day.
    d. Practice time should vary, according to the difficulty of the class' repertoire and the student's mood.

77. A choir teacher composes a suite of music with her class and feels the music is of sufficient quality to copyright. What must she do to protect it?
    a. Record it.
    b. Have it published.
    c. Have it registered with the Copyright Office.
    d. Perform it publicly.

78. Which of the following is true of crescendo and decrescendo?
    a. Percussion and upper voices should decrescendo more quickly than lower voices.
    b. Percussion should play the entire crescendo at an even, proportionally louder rate.
    c. Ensembles should play crescendos at an even, proportionally louder rate.
    d. Lower voices should crescendo more slowly than upper voices.

79. Which of the following is true of the manner in which instrumental ensembles should be organized?
    a. First chair players should be kept far from each other so that they may better hear themselves play.
    b. Cornet I and Trumpet I should sit far from each other so that they may better hear themselves play.
    c. Tenor saxophones should sit near the euphoniums, as they often play the same tenor line.
    d. Students should maximize limited music stand resources by sitting three or more to a stand.

80. A high school choir travels via school bus to a neighboring town for a festival. After the performance, one of the student musicians asks the band director if she can ride home in a car driven by her brother, who is a freshman in college. A second student asks if he can drive home with friends from school. A third asks if she can ride home with her parents. Following best practices, students should be allowed to travel home by which of the following means other than the school bus?
    a. None of the students should be allowed to ride home by any means other than the school bus.
    b. All three students should be allowed to travel home on their own if they have arranged it ahead of time with the band director and parents approve in writing   and sign a waiver.
    c. Only the student traveling home with her parents; the other two students should take the bus back to their school.
    d. All family members should be considered safe transport, as the student is covered under the family's insurance; traveling home with friends is unacceptable.

- 93 -

81. What is the role of a standard written exam for student musicians? (That is, a written exam that includes true-false, multiple choice, and essay questions?)
    a. There is no role for the standard written exam in musical education.
    b. To test only beginning students; more advanced and older students should be free to rehearse and perform only.
    c. To test concepts such as time and key signatures, music symbols, and musical history.
    d. Only to satisfy the school's requirement that all students receive a letter grade for all classes.

82. Competitions for chair positions in a student band or orchestra:
    a. should be held daily
    b. have no place in a the rehearsal space of an enlightened music educator in charge of developing musicians' self-esteem
    c. should be held at the beginning and end of the semester only
    d. should be held both unannounced and on a scheduled basis, at the instructor's discretion

83. The most common method of vibrato for trumpet—and the easiest to develop—is
    a. voice vibrato
    b. hand vibrato
    c.jaw vibrato
    d. embouchure vibrato

84. The average school concert band should be comprised of approximately
    a. half woodwinds and half brass, balanced equally
    b. one third woodwind and two thirds brass
    c. two thirds woodwinds and one third brass
    d. mostly brass; as long as it's fifty percent or more, the sound will be fine for a   student ensemble

85. A band director is blessed with a group of eager, committed beginning musicians, all of whom have their hearts set on their instruments of choice. In fact, most of the students have already rented or purchased these instruments, and few, if any, can be persuaded to switch to other instruments in order to allow the band to have the proper brass-to-woodwinds balance. The band director then should
    a. call a parents' meeting and explain the situation, in the hopes that the parents can persuade their children to change
    b. establish a "cut" list, the way sports teams do, in order to achieve the proper ratio
    c. use peer pressure to get students to persuade their band mates to switch instruments
    d. make changes to the music, moving some instruments to other instruments' parts, as long as the central integrity of the music is preserved

86. Which of the following would be an appropriate adaptation for a student musician identified as a gifted and talented learner?
    a. Allowing them to learn music by ear, as gifted students tend to be more intuitive.
    b. Separating them into classes apart from their more "average" peers.
    c. Independent projects, such as composition and improvisation.
    d. There should be no adaptations, as gifted learners adapt well to any classroom.

87. Which of the following is true for hearing-impaired music students?
    a. They are required by federal law to have an aide with them at all times, especially in music classes.
    b. Their disability precludes them from taking music classes, especially if that disability is severe.
    c. It is best if they are limited to kinesthetic instruments, such as percussion.
    d. A music teacher is permitted to make other accommodations, even beyond those outlined in the student's Individualized Education Plan (IEP).

88. Which of the following is true about the Suzuki method of musical instruction?
    a. It places a primary emphasis on teaching sight-reading and musical notation.
    b. It is used only for students studying guitar and piano.
    c. It was developed in the United States by a Japanese immigrant.
    d. It deliberately avoids auditions as a means of judging suitability for instruction.

89. Which of the following musical instruction methods holds that all aspiring musicians, even instrumentalists, should begin their instruction through singing?
    a. Dalcroze
    b. Kodály
    c. Orff Schulwerk
    d. Suzuki

90. According to state music safety guidelines, what is required of instrument mouthpieces that are shared between students?
    a. Mouthpieces should be sterilized before being shared.
    b. Mouthpieces should never be shared under any circumstances.
    c. There are no guidelines for sharing mouthpieces.
    d. Most mouthpieces are self-sterilizing; there has never been a documented case off disease transmission through shared mouthpieces.

91. Which of the following is *not* a stage of the Americanized version of the Orff-Schulwerk process?
    a. imitation
    b. exploration
    c. composition
    d. improvisation

92. Which of the following statements is true of teaching gospel music in public schools?
    a. As long as songs that avoid outright Biblical passages and themes are avoided or minimized, gospel music emphasizing broader themes (love, freedom, etc.) can be a included as part of a public school's music curriculum.
    b. The U.S. Supreme Court has ruled that singing gospel music of any kind in music classes violates separation of church and state.
    c. Because it is "culturally significant," gospel music can be taught by specialists who do not hold a current teaching license.
    d. Because it is regarded as a "European-American" genre, gospel has no place in a modern, multicultural curriculum.

93. The standout trumpeter in a high school concert band lately has been making obvious mistakes and throwing off the ensemble during rehearsals. The director strongly suspects that she has not been practicing. What would be an appropriate intervention?

a. Ask the student to perform her piece in front of the entire group, and say that she will be doing so for the next week.

b. Confer with the student privately about the importance of practice, and warn her that her top spot could slip in an upcoming trial for first chair.

c. Nothing; these things have a way of working themselves out.

d. Levy consequences to the entire trumpet section, in the hopes that they will apply peer pressure to their first chair.

94. According to The National Association for Music Education standards for music teachers, which grade level's students might be assessed in their singing of the song "America the Beautiful"?

a. Pre-Kindergarten

b. K-4

c. 5-8

d. 9-12

95. According to standards set forth for music teachers, beginning music teachers working with children from early childhood to fourth grade (EC-4) should:

a. have an advanced music degree from an accredited institution

b. be able to sing or play a musical instrument

c. be at least 25 years old

d. have performed professionally, i.e. on a paying basis for at least six months

96. When accused of substantial wrongdoing in a classroom or other setting involving students, when should a teacher admit liability?

a. never

b. if ordered to do so by an administrator

c. if doing so will mean the problem can be resolved

d. when talking to the media

97. Which of the following statements is true of a *diagnostic* assessment?

a. It is performed at the beginning of the semester, and it includes auditions.

b. It is performed in the middle of the semester, and is an important component of a student musician's midterm letter grade.

c. It is another term for summative assessment.

d. It never should be reserved for students college age and above.

98. Students with overbites tend to play with their brass instruments pointed downward, which hurts their sound and can affect their posture. Which of the following statements offers an acceptable way for a band teacher to correct this problem?

a. Teach the student to bend his or her wrists to compensate.

b. Require that all horn players have a more "normal" bite or be under the care of an orthodontist.

c. The teacher should accept that students play differently; the orientation of the instrument should not affect its tone or volume.

d. Suggest that the student move the jaw forward comfortably.

99. Which of the following assessment scales would be appropriate for a teacher measuring progress of her second grade music students?
    a. letter grades, A to F
    b. percentages
    c. second graders are too young for assessments; the focus should be on an introduction to music without judgment or pressure
    d. a simple system such as checks and plusses

100. Which of the following styles of music would feature taiko drums?
    a. Navajo
    b. Chinese
    c. West African
    d. Japanese

Constructed Response

You attend a chamber music concert at a local university and are asked to critique the first-year music students' performance. In detail, describe your process of interpretation, including which aspects of the performance you would consider in your critique and how highly you would rank those aspects in importance. Discuss common errors that occur during a musical performance given by beginner students and how these problems could be addressed by an instructor.

Answers and Explanations

1. **A:** With the chord of C major being composed of the notes C, E, and G. C is the root of the chord, E forms the major third, and G forms the perfect fifth. Answer B, by flatting the major third of E to E ♭, changes the chord to a C minor. Answer C includes the seventh note of B, creating a C major seventh. By flatting the third, to E ♭and adding the seventh note B, Answer D creates a C minor seventh.

2. **B:** There is a note between every natural note on the scale except B and C, and E and F. In Western music, sharps and flats lie between most of the notes on the scale. For example, between the notes C and D, one would find the note C # (or D ♭); the sharps and flats on a piano keyboard are indicated by the black keys. The only place on the chromatic scale—which includes *all* notes—where one wouldn't find sharps and flats would be between the notes B and C, and E and F. There is no "B #/C ♭," nor is there an "E #/ F ♭."

3. **B:** B ♭. clarinets come in different lengths, and to facilitate ease of playing in transposing instruments, the same fingering will produce a different tone on different lengths of instruments. Otherwise, players would have to learn different fingerings. Clarinets avoid this by transposing different notes. A clarinetist on a B ♭ instrument would finger the note C, but would produce the note B ♭. A B ♭ clarinet transposes the note C into B ♭, by definition.

4. **A:** C in a first inversion, the lowest note in the chord's root position—C, in this case—would be moved up a full octave, thereby inverting the chord. Moving up E—answer B—would create a second inversion, while moving up G in choice C—provided the other notes had been moved up as well—would create the same chord, only an octave higher.

5. **D:** The twelfth bar. In the twelve-bar blues form (also jazz) the turnaround refers to the passage at the end of one section that leads to the next section. Twelve-bar compositions are typically arranged with the first four measures under the I chord. The next four measures are split typically between the IV chord and the I chord. The final set of four bars leads to some combination of the I, IV, and V chords, which compels the listener to "turnaround" to another set of twelve bars. Given that the turnaround would come at the end of the collection of measures, answers A through C would, by definition, be incorrect.

6. **C:** In 3/4 time, the quarter note is selected as the one beat unit, while in 6/8 time the eighth note is used. Essentially, 6/8 time is the same as the six-note form of 3/4. The only difference is that the eighth note is used as the one-beat unit.

7. **C:** Allegro, which uses a tempo between 120 and 168 beats per minute (bpm). While Allegro can be thought of as a "quick" tempo, it is not as fast as Presto, played between 168 and 200 bpm. Therefore, answer A is incorrect. Moderato and Largo—played between 108-120 and 40-60, respectively—are slower tempos, proving answers B and D incorrect.

8. **A:** The distinctive music used for the movie *Jaws* whenever the shark appears or is nearby. By definition, a *leitmotif* is a distinctive musical theme or melody associated with a particular story element such as a character or place. The shark's theme in *Jaws* would be a classic example. Answers B through D describe the terms *concerto, chromatic modulation,* and *libretto,* respectively.

9. B: A major, in whose scale the notes C, F, and G are the sharps. Answer A, D major, would have a key signature featuring two sharps, F and C, so that answer is incorrect. Answer C, G major, has one sharp, the note F; therefore this answer is incorrect. Pieces composed in C have neither sharps nor flats indicated. Note: The other key signature to display three sharp symbols would be F # minor. Each major key signature has a corresponding minor key.

10. B: Faster than Andante but slower than Moderato. The tempo of this piece is listed above and to the right in italics with the word Andantino, which means faster than Andante (76 to 108 beats per minute) but slower than Moderato, which is typically understood to mean 108 to 120 beats per minute.

11. B: Mazurka. One clue to this correct answer would be the composer, Frédéric Chopin, who wrote fifty-eight of them. Another clue would be the fact that the mazurka is a Polish dance, and Chopin was Polish. Additionally, the music itself offers many clues. Mazurkas predominantly are written in 3/4 time and always are structured with a triplet, trill, dotted pair of eighth notes, or an ordinary eighth note pair, right before two quarter notes. While the polka is often associated with Poland, it is actually a Czech dance with a 2/4 time signature. Thus, answer A is incorrect. Also incorrect would be answer C, an dro, a Breton folk dance with also is played in 2/4 time. Rounding out the list of two-beat folk dances is incorrect answer D, the kolo, which originated in the Balkans.

12. A: Legato. The curved lines indicate that the notes on the upper staves should be played smoothly without silence in between; *legato* is Italian for "tied together." Answer B, staccato, is incorrect, since staccato playing is the exact opposite of legato. Staccato is indicated by a dot either above or below each note. Answers C and D refer to terms indicating the relative loudness of how the piece is to be played. Fortissimo, indicated by *ff*, is a piece played extremely loudly; mezzo piano, *mp*, means a piece that is played moderately softly. The piece is indeed labeled *mp*, but this has nothing to do with the curved lines over the notes. Therefore, answer D is also incorrect.

13. B: Compound intervals. An interval is the number of steps between two notes, and calling an interval a "compound interval" denotes the number of spaces greater than an octave, the point at which notes would begin recurring. For example, a "tenth" would be known as a "compound third." Answer A, octave intervals, is not a term used in music composition. Answer C, perfect fifths, refers to an interval of 3:2, less than the span of an octave. Answer D is incorrect, as intervals larger than an octave are quite common in music.

14. B: Because they lack a tonal center. For example, diminished triads consisting of a root, a minor third, and a diminished fifth symmetrically divide the octave. Answer A is incorrect, since diminished chords do not necessarily sound "sad" depending on their placement in the chord progression (minor chords typically are considered "sad," anyway). Answer C, they are barely audible, is incorrect, as the word "diminished" refers to the state of the fifth and not the volume of the chord, which can be played at any volume. Finally, Answer D is incorrect, as diminished chords have been used throughout musical history in many famous works.

15. C: "Pictures at an Exhibition" by Modest Mussorgsky. The answer cannot be A, since "The Blue Danube," one of history's most famous waltzes, is in 3/4 time. Bach's fifth Brandenburg Concerto is in 4/4 time, so answer B is incorrect, as would Claude Debussy's "Claire de Lune," answer d. Only answer C, "Pictures at an Exhibition," is in the asymmetrical meters of 5/4 and 6/4 time, or five beats and six per measure, respectively, in which the quarter note acts as the one-beat unit.

16. A: B-flat major. The key of B-flat major is designated by two ♭symbols next to both the treble and bass clefs. The key of C-sharp major, answer B, has seven sharp symbols next to the clefs, so that is incorrect.

Also incorrect would be answer C, A-flat minor, has seven flat symbols next to the clefs. The key of C major, answer D, has no flat or sharp symbols next to the clefs, and therefore this answer also is correct.

17. B: Ostinato, an Italian term meaning "obstinate" or "stubborn." This term refers to a musical phrase or theme that is repeated over and over throughout a piece. All of the examples listed, either in their bass lines or in their melodies, repeat the same phrase for most or all of the song. The term solfège, answer B, refers to the practice of assigning a syllable to each musical note, and is incorrect. Also incorrect is answer C, tessitura, which most commonly refers to a singer's most comfortable range; and answer D, pizzicato, which refers to the practice of plucking musical instruments, particularly those that are usually played with a bow.

18. B: 2:1. Both notes are G, separated by one octave. An octave is the interval between two notes, where the higher note's frequency is exactly twice that of the lower. Answer A, 1:1, is incorrect, because obviously the notes are not the same. One is higher than the other and therefore has a higher frequency. Answers C and D are both incorrect, since a frequency ratio of 4:1 or 8:1 refers to differences of two and three octaves, respectively.

19. C: 4/4 time. Right before the first measure, the piece indicates a large "C" in place of a traditional fractional time signature. The C stands for "common time." Common time indicates 4/4 time, the most common time signature in Western music, in which each measure contains 4 beats. Had the time signature been 2/2, or "cut time," the symbol also would have been a large C, but with a vertical slash, similar to the monetary symbol for "cent." Therefore, answer A is incorrect. Also incorrect is answer B, 3/4 time, indicated with a 3/4 symbol, as is answer D, 5/4 time, indicated by a 5/4 symbol.

20. B: Fugue. A fugue is a piece of music opening with an exposition or "subject," and then answering in subsequent measures by the "countersubject." In this piece, Bach's "Little Fugue in G minor," the subject plays for five measures and then in answered in measure six by the countersubject, a different melody built on the same theme. In this piece, when the countersubject begins, the notes on the bass part take over the role of the subject. Answers A and D, sonata and cantata, are incorrect choices for this answer. The cantata form generally features the vocals, while the sonata features instrumental performances. (The lack of lyrics would be a strong clue that this is not a choral piece.) A gigue, answer C, is a lively, Baroque-era dance. It is usually written in a 3/8 time signature. Gigues rarely were written in 4/4 time, and since this piece is in common, or 4/4 time, answer C is incorrect.

21. A: Trill. A trill is the rapid alternation between two notes, usually adjacent to each other. If the piece had called for a tie between all of the notes in the rest of the measure (unlikely, since different notes are seen) they would have been grouped together with an arcing line. Therefore, answer B is incorrect. Also incorrect is answer C, tenuto, which means either to play a given note slightly louder or slightly longer than is indicated, and usually is shown in musical notation with a short bar above the note in question. A turn, answer D, is incorrect, since it calls for short sequence consisting of the note above the one indicated, the original note, the note below, and the note itself again. It is shown with a horizontal "S" shape, not a "tr" symbol, and is also an incorrect answer.

22. C: Subject. It may be tempting, if one recognizes this piece as a fugue, to label the appearance of the alto notes as the piece's countersubject, since in this piece the subject is introduced at the very beginning. Yet, the countersubject introduced in measure six is being played by the higher notes, while the subject is now being replayed by the lower ones. Therefore, answer D, countersubject, would be incorrect. Also incorrect is answer A, coda, since a coda refers to the section of a musical composition that brings the piece to a close; even if the excerpt above were the entire piece, measure six is near the center. The

featured excerpt is the introduction to a longer piece of music (Bach's *Little Fugue in G minor)*, so the middle entry, answer B, is also incorrect.

23. D: Johannes Brahms, who composed music in the middle to late 19th century. Therefore, Brahms is most strongly associated with the Romantic Period in classical music, which ran from about 1815 to about 1910. Bach is most strongly associated with the Baroque Period (1600-1760), and Ravel is most closely associated with the Impressionist Period (1890-1940). Choice D, Aaron Copland, often is considered "the dean of American composers" and composed music in the mid to late 20th century; he would not fit into any of the above listed periods.

24. B: To create a style of art music that was uniquely and characteristically Russian. The group aimed to produce a specifically Russian kind of art music, rather than a style imitating older European music or relying upon European-style conservatory training. As such, these composers would have eschewed excessive imitation of Western European forms, so answer A is incorrect. The musicians listed were not particularly famous for bringing music to the poor, nor were they known for challenging the ruling royal families of Russia. Accordingly, answers C and D are also incorrect.

25. A: Tango, traditionally played to accompany its distinctive style of dance. Salsa, Flamenco, and Tejano music have varying influences and, as such, use a wide variety of instruments in their performance. Only Tango music is strongly associated with the specific combination of two violins, a piano, double bass, and two bandoneóns.

26. D: Bebop's use of asymmetrical phrasing and an expanded role for the rhythm section. Benny Goodman and Glenn Miller typified traditional jazz of the "Swing" era. While traditional jazz was easy to follow for the casual listener and often danceable, bebop was instead characterized by quicker tempos, intricate if not chaotic melodies, and rhythm sections that were called upon to do more than keep the beat for the ensemble's other musicians. Many jazz bands—even traditional jazz bands—were integrated by the 1940s, when Bebop had its genesis, so answer A is incorrect. Also, answer C is incorrect, since bebop produced many famous horn players. The complicated and unexpected rhythms associated with this style of jazz make answer B—strict adherence to a 4/4 time signature—obviously incorrect.

27. D: Ewe. The Ewe culture is West African and has a folk musical form based primarily on drums played with complex rhythms and meter. All of the other answers, A, B, and C, are incorrect, since they use many musical instruments in addition to percussion instruments. Finnish music, for example, uses instruments such as the harmonium, flute, and fiddle. Peruvian music predominantly features its iconic flutes and the charango, a type of mandolin. Mongolian folk music is famous for its use of the *morin khuur*, or horse-head fiddle. Therefore, of forms listed above, only Ewe is an appropriate answer.

28. C: Flutes. The earliest flutes are thought to have been made from hollowed bones with drilled finger holes. Archaeologists have found many examples, many of which are still playable. While the age of the oldest flutes is a topic of debate, the oldest flute upon which historians can agree may be as much as 37,000 years old. By contrast, trumpets, answer A, require the ability to smith metal such as bronze or brass; the oldest specimens date to about 1500 Bc. Therefore, answer A is incorrect. Also incorrect is answer B; violins' ancient, plucked ancestors (such as the lyre) go back at most a few thousand years, and did not emerge in their modern form until the 16th century in Italy. Answer D, xylophones, is also incorrect, since the earliest documented instruments resembling their modern form did not appear in China until about 2000 Bc.

29. A: U.S. churches in the 1930s. Laurens Hammond developed this instrument in 1934 and marketed it to churches as a low-cost alternative to the large and expensive pipe organs then used for religious

services. The Hammond organ emerged after the Baroque period; therefore, answer C is incorrect. Answer D is incorrect for the same reason. Finally, while the Hammond did in fact see widespread use with popular musicians starting in the 1960s, jazz, blues, and other performers were not the instrument's original market. Widespread Hammond use among jazz, blues, and other performers did not emerge until the instrument had been on the market for almost thirty years.

30. C: A Bach fugue, which would not be described as monophonic, or using one and only one melodic voice at a time. Gregorian chants, therapeutic songs of Indian classical music, and most of the songs sung by troubadours in the Middle Ages, were all constructed monophonically. Because a fugue necessarily has two or more "voices" being performed at once, it is described as polyphonic, and thus the only correct answer from this list.

31. B: Harpsichord. The harpsichord is a piano-like instrument, which, unlike a piano, produces sound when the keys activate a plectrum, which, in turn, plucks a string. The clavichord produces sound when a similar mechanism strikes iron or brass strings with a small metal blade, so answer A is incorrect. Also incorrect is answer C, the piano. A piano produces sounds when its strings are struck by a hammer. The final answer, D, hurdy gurdy, would be incorrect because a hurdy gurdy produces its sounds through a complex combination of wheel, strings, and keyboard.

32. C: Joaquin Rodrigo. Unusual in its placement of the guitar as a stand-alone against the full force of an orchestra, *Concerto de Aranjuez* is one of the most recognizable pieces written for the instrument. Although Fernando Sor is known in Spain as "the Beethoven of the classical guitar" for his important contribution to the instrument, he died in 1839, one hundred years before Rodrigo wrote *Concerto de Aranjuez*. That would make answer A incorrect. While master guitarist Manuel Barrueco has performed arguably the most celebrated recording of the concerto, he did not write it. Therefore, answer B is incorrect. Finally, answer D, famed composer and guitarist Francisco Tárrega, is incorrect as well, since he died in 1909.

33. A: Call and response. Indeed, the phrase *kan ha diskan* can be translated from the Breton language as "call and response," and is performed unaccompanied by a lead singer (a *kaner*) and a secondary singer (a *diskaner*). The correct answer to this question is necessarily very specific, so an instrumental, non vocal form such as chamber music, answer C, is incorrect. *Kan ha diskan* generally is not considered microtonal, or moving freely between Western music's established notes, so answer C is incorrect. Again, because *kan ha diskan* is unaccompanied by any instrument outside the human voice, answer D, percussion only, is incorrect.

34. A: *Fiddler on the Roof,* a musical that follows the struggles of a Jewish father trying to keep his faith and traditions alive. Klezmer, a Jewish musical tradition and form often performed with instruments such as the clarinet, accordion, and piano, is featured predominantly in the musical. As none of the other answers—B, *The Sound of Music,* C, *Oklahoma!,* or D, *A Chorus Line*—is necessarily a celebration of Jewish culture, heritage, or music, none of these are correct.

35. C: Sir Arthur Sullivan. While both operas and operettas involve actors on a stage singing their lines to a musical score, operetta generally is lighter in tone and substance than its weightier cousin. One of the most well-known composers of operettas is Sir Arthur Sullivan, who, with his collaborator, Sir William Gilbert, wrote fourteen operettas, including *The Pirates of Penzance* and *H.M.S. Pinafore.* Answer A, Wolfgang Amadeus Mozart; B, Giacomo Puccini; and D, Giuseppe Verdi; were all composers of opera rather than operetta and therefore incorrect answers.

36. B: "Rapper's Delight" by The Sugarhill Gang. While not the first rap single, "Rapper's Delight" was the first hip hop song to enjoy widespread airplay across the United States. Rap went on to become one of the most important—if not **the** most important—urban and youth musical genres starting in the 1980s and continuing to the present day. "Rapper's Delight" was released in 1979, predating all of the other examples in this list. "Walk This Way," recorded jointly by Run-d.M.c. and Aerosmith in 1986, was immensely popular and vaulted Run-d.M.c. into rap music's pantheon, but is incorrect because of its later release date. Also debuting after 1979—"Hit 'Em Up" in 1996 and "Don't Believe the Hype" in 1988— answers C and D, respectively, are incorrect.

37. B: Women. *Castrati* were male singers castrated before the onset of puberty could deepen their voices. A few *castrati* went on to fame and fortune as soloists, but most sang the higher parts in religious ensembles, as women had been forbidden from performing by papal edict. Protestants obviously were not banned from performing religious music, so answer A is incorrect, as is answer C, commoners, as they filled many musical performing roles throughout the history of Western classical music, both religious and secular. Finally, as boys were also valued for their high voices and often sang in church choirs, answer D is incorrect.

38. D: German music. The word *Tejano* refers to someone from Texas of Latino and/or Hispanic descent. While Tejano music has strong cultural ties to neighboring Mexico, it also draws a heavy influence from the music of German and Czech settlers in the region. Europeans brought with them musical elements such as the polka, accordion, and waltz. Fusing these with styles such as mariachi gradually resulted in Tejano music. While it might be tempting to choose Peruvian music, answer A, for this question, Peru's distinctive Incan roots have nothing to do with influencing Tejano music, nor does African or Celtic music. For this reason, answers A, B, and C are incorrect.

39. C: MP3 removes selected information, including frequencies from the original file too low or too high for humans to hear. This process results in a lower-quality recording small enough for storage en masse on computers and/or MP3 players. Shrinking the file size is key to converting a file to MP3, but this shrinking cannot be achieved by recording at a lower volume, so answer A is incorrect. Copying a file with selected vocal or instrumental tracks removed is not the idea of MP3, so converting the digital information to analog, would be incorrect.

40. B: The use of the third. Prior to the Renaissance, the use of the third was regarded as dissonant, but with increased vocal range gradually began to be used as consonance. The use of the second always has been considered dissonant in Western music, so answer A is incorrect. Also incorrect is answer C, the fifth, which was used as consonance more toward the end of the Renaissance and the beginning of the Baroque. Finally, because intervals had been used long before the Renaissance, answer D is incorrect.

41. C: Gong. The gong is integral to Indonesian *gamelan* ensemble music, integral to Indonesian life and culture. Indeed, the word *gamelan* means "to hit" or "to hammer," and while gamelan can include instruments as flutes and bowed or plucked strings, the gong is central to the form. All of the other choices are stringed instruments from around the Eastern Hemisphere. Answer A, the bulbul tarang, is an Indian stringed instrument similar to a banjo, and therefore is incorrect. Also incorrect is answer B, the qinqin, another stringed instrument from China. Finally, the kora, a 12-string harp lute from West Africa, is incorrect.

42. C: The course of a river as it winds through Central Europe. The Vltava is the longest river running through the area now classified as the Czech Republic, and the suite by the same name about his native land is part of a larger work titled *Má Vlast* by Czech composer Bedřich Smetana . The defeat of invading French armies, answer A, is the subject of Pyotr Ilyich Tchaikovsky's *1812 Overture*. Answer B, concerning

the king and his trolls, concerns Edvard Grieg's *In the Hall of the Mountain King.* Answer D, the audio tour of a symphony, is *The Young Person's Guide to the Orchestra* by Benjamin Britten.

43. D: Pyotr Ilyich Tchaikovsky and Edvard Grieg. Grieg and Tchaikovsky lived and composed during the same time period, the mid- to late 19th century, and, in the case of Grieg, into the early 20th. Indeed, they met in 1888. The rest of the composers that form the answers to this question did not live during the same eras and therefore never could have met. In the case of answer incorrect answer A, Vivaldi died in 1741, while Chopin was not born until 1810. Answer B is incorrect, since Holst was not born until 1874, 124 years after the death of Bach. Finally, Pachelbel died in 1706, 105 years before the birth of Liszt.

44. C: The Romantic period. Partly as a response to the widely perceived dominance of German music and composers during the Classical period that preceded it, the Romantic period is most strongly associated with musical nationalism; that is, composers from a given nation wrote music meant to invoke their native lands, peoples, and cultures. Noted examples include the music of Bedřich Smetana, Antonín Dvořák, and Jean Sibelius. While the other periods—Baroque, Classical, and Contemporary—would have seen selected composers and pieces which could be argued as nationalistic, the Romantic period *most strongly* is associated with musical nationalism and is therefore the correct answer.

45. D: Choosing a violin that allows the student's fingers to curl comfortably around the scroll, with the elbow slightly bent. While taller children and teens tend to have longer arms, arm lengths vary even among students of the same height, so the method described by answer A is ineffective. Answer B is also incorrect, since student musicians are still learning proper technique and may not yet have a feel for the best instrument. A violin that extends to the base of a student's hand (Answer C) would be too small. This process of elimination leaves answer D, which would yield an instrument that allows the student to hold and play the violin comfortably.

46. C: Concerts B♭ and F, with the exception of saxophones. Concert B♭ is a good tuning note for the majority of instruments, as it is well within their range. Concert F is excellent for horns, and in fact is better than B♭, and also is excellent for clarinets. Nonetheless, these concert pitches are not suitable for tuning saxophones.

47. D: Criminal fines up to $250,000 and/or a five-year sentence. The penalties are extremely severe for educators who photocopy music or commit other copyright infringement for personal monetary gain. Copyright law is strict, even in an age music content and sheet music often appears free for the taking. While companies are given the discretion to warn teachers in writing, answer A, they do have the option of pursuing more severe penalties. So, answer A is incorrect for a maximum penalty. Both two years' probation, answer B, and the unspecified statutory damages of $750 to $30,000 are incorrect, because they do not refer to the maximum penalty a teacher can face if he or she chooses to violate copyright protection for personal gain.

48. B: One copy. Voluntary guidelines allow for one and exactly one recording of student work, as long as it is used for educational or archival purposes. Beyond that, a license is required. Obviously, answer A, which would permit anyone to make as many copies of performances as they wished, would be in violation of copyright law. For this reason, answers C and D would be incorrect as well, since one and only one copy is permitted without paying a licensing fee.

49. A: A choir director may rearrange, edit, or simplify copyrighted material, so long as he or she retains the fundamental character of the piece and neither adds nor changes lyrics. Copyright law is clear on this matter, spelling out exactly what educators' rights are in this area, so answers C and D are incorrect.

Licensing fees permit a choral or band director only limited arranging rather than fundamental changes, so answer B is incorrect.

50. C: Do nothing since his role as a teacher allows this type of presentation. Under Section 110 of the copyright code, a teacher is granted a "face-to-face" exemption from having to seek or pay for performance rights, provided the music is intended for an educational setting in the physical presence of students. Since this right is stated explicitly in the code, answer A is incorrect, since the teacher is not required to seek or pay for permission from a licensing group. He or she also is allowed to present the music to students without paying for the rights, which makes answer B incorrect. Since copyright code explicitly permits such use, answer D is incorrect in all cases like this one.

51. A: Require the student to play in the low register and then activate the register key. Doing so should allow the student automatically to cross into the higher register, divided from the beginning, lower registers by "the break," which can intimidate beginning clarinetists. Blowing with more force, answer B, merely will result in a louder, incorrect tone, and is an incorrect answer to this question. Answer C, requiring the student to play through "the break" scale wise, is an overly difficult and intimidating method, so answer C is incorrect. Answer D, relying less on the throat registers, is incorrect, since mastery of the throat registers is an important fundamental skill for any clarinetist before upper registers can be attained.

52. C: It should only be used for keeping the horn steady while turning pages or inserting a mute. Trumpet players may be tempted to hook their little fingers in the ring while playing, but often the little finger is needed to support the weak ring finger in pressing valves. Therefore, answer A is incorrect. Because the ring finger is the primary finger used for depressing the third valve, answer B is incorrect. Also incorrect is answer D, since modern trumpets in fact are manufactured with a finger ring.

53. C: A timpani has a normal compass of a perfect fifth. Although a timpani can be stretched to a minor sixth, this would require the use of plastic heads. As such, all of the other answers would be incorrect. Answers A and B, a minor third and a perfect fourth, require a smaller compass than that permitted by a timpani; a major seventh is too large, even with an instrument fitted with plastic heads.

54. A: Brass valves should be oiled once a day. Doing so keeps the valves in good working order, and prevents sticking and damage to the valve mechanism. Once per week is incorrect, as the valves will need lubrication before a week has elapsed, so B is incorrect. Also incorrect is C, once a month; it is doubtful that a brass instrument played with any regularity, could go a full month without some oiling. Waiting until the valves begin to stick, answer D, is incorrect, since sticking valves can disrupt a rehearsal, practice, or, worse, a performance, and should be oiled regularly to prevent this from occurring.

55. B: Hitting notes on a xylophone with the correct rhythm. The word *kinesthetic* pertains to physical activity or movement, and this kind of activity is especially valuable within the context of learning. Learning to read musical notation by listening to music might be valuable, but it would not involve the child moving around or connecting his or her body movements to rhythm. So, answer A is incorrect, as are answers C or D, which would, again, satisfy musical or interpersonal learning goals, but not kinesthetic learning goals.

56. C: The viola uses the alto or "viola" clef, which is rarely used for other instruments or compositions. To the untrained eye, the viola is easily mistaken for its smaller cousin, the violin, but many differences exist between the instruments. The viola is tuned a perfect fifth below the violin, and whereas the violin's four strings are tuned to GDAE, the viola's tuning is CGDa. Therefore, answer A is incorrect. While the viola is indeed a mainstay of most symphony orchestras, it is also an integral part of most chamber pieces,

rendering answer B incorrect. In addition, the viola is larger than the violin *and* it uses a correspondingly larger bow, which is also wider than that of the violin. Therefore, answer D is incorrect.

57. B: 415 Hz. The frequency is a half step lower than 440A, the almost universally accepted pitch for modern performance. Baroque musicians are thought to have performed tuned to an A somewhere in the vicinity of 415, which is now called "Baroque pitch." Answer A, 220 Hz, would correspond to an A3 tone, and would be almost an octave below Baroque pitch. Therefore, answer A is incorrect. Answer C is, of course, the modern 440A pitch, or A4. It is incorrect, as is 880 Hz, answer D, which corresponds to an A5.

58. D: It indicates the fingering position, note for note, of pieces for stringed instruments. Tablatures are popular with beginning musicians, particularly those attempting to learn their favorite songs on the guitar. With a numbering system that bears some resemblance to a traditional staff, tablature indicates by number where the player should place his or her fingers on a fret and string, note for note. Because many online sharing networks of tabs offer them free of charge, music publishers have declared them illegal, and the courts are still undecided regarding whether tab providers are violating copyright laws. Therefore, answer A is incorrect. Also incorrect is answer b. While tab does show a beginning musician where to play his or her fingers to produce a given note or chord, using tab does not allow him or her to learn key signature, tempo, or other skills necessary to learn mastery of an instrument. For this reason, answer C also is incorrect.

59. A: At the beginning of class. While all of a vocal performance class should be considered voice training, all classes should start with warm-ups. During this time, teachers should reinforce the fundamentals of singing, such as breath and posture, range, and intonation. Because the quality of student singing is likely to be poor without adequate preparation, answer B is incorrect, as is answer C, as an entire class period of poorly performed pieces would make the vocal training at the end of class largely moot. Since most students in a general classroom setting do not receive private voice training and are in classes, ostensibly, to obtain such training, answer D is incorrect. Indeed, all young singers can benefit from the fundamentals of voice training, regardless of whether or not they are taking private lessons.

60. D: Girls' singing voices change just as boys' do. While the change may begin earlier—as is the case with most of a girl's adolescent development—and is subtler, it does indeed take place. Girls who wish to sing through early adolescence and beyond will need the coaching of a good, patient instructor. Because girls' voices change, answers A and B are incorrect. Also incorrect is answer c. Boys, like girls, can make good music in elementary and middle school, regardless of the changes taking place in their voices.

61. C: The oboe uses a double reed. The oboe, along with the bassoon, uses a double reed system to produce its distinctive sound. While playing the instrument can present a challenge to younger, more inexperienced players, it is possible for a student in even in the elementary grades to begin playing the oboe with a little extra help from his or her teacher. Only if extra time is impossible should an aspiring oboist be guided toward the clarinet or saxophone first. Therefore, answer A is incorrect. Also incorrect is answer B, because an oboe properly played should be held between 30 and 45 degrees from the body. Finally, since the oboe is assembled in four parts, not three, answer D is incorrect.

62. D: Program notes should include the names of the arrangers of instrumental and vocal pieces, not just the names of composers. In addition, more complete program notes could provide brief information about the music contained in the program in order to give the audience a greater understanding and appreciation for the musical selections they are about to hear. As such, answer A, that notes are optional, is incorrect. Answer B is also incorrect, since notes showing only the names and composers of the pieces are incomplete in almost all performances. While program notes certainly should engage the audience,

excessively long notes containing pages of information or song lyrics would be too much for most audiences and not add anything to the performance.

63. A: Sitting toward the back of the seat with the back touching the backrest. Proper sitting posture dictates that the student's back should be straight and away from the chair's backrest. All of the rest of the answers, answers B, C, and D, respectively, with feet apart, body in line, and chest lifted, all constitute *correct* posture, and therefore are *incorrect* answers for this question.

64. C: Feet together. When standing for a choir rehearsal or performance, the feet should be shoulder width apart. Keeping the feet together as stated in the question will lead to improper balance. All of the rest of the elements, answers A, B, and D, respectively, with knees relaxed, body in line, and chest lifted, etc., all constitute *correct* standing posture, and therefore are *incorrect* answers for this question.

65. C: Teachers should have at least a passing familiarity with all of the instruments in the bands they are teaching. While teachers cannot be expected to play every instrument with skill, finesse, and grace, they should have enough familiarity with each instrument at least to engage beginning students and help them through the early stages of playing. Fortunately, quality undergraduate music programs offer methods and or pedagogy courses in order to familiarize their students with a wide range of instruments, which will serve to help future music teachers. To fill in the gaps of their knowledge, band teachers should enlist the help of guest musicians or local music students whenever possible. Answer A is incorrect, since all band teachers obviously need to be proficient in at least one instrument and acquainted with the other instruments in order to be successful in the classroom; state standards require this for certification. Answer B is for this reason, as successful band teachers need to be familiar with all instruments. While answer D would be ideal, this level of proficiency and skill simply is not realistic for all band directors.

66. C: The flute player should be encouraged to tap her toe inside her shoe, because a little motion is fine. Indeed, some professional symphony players are known to tap their feet during performances, so some visible motion certainly acceptable. Still, overt motion, especially if such motion is excessive, can be distracting during a performance, so answer A, doing nothing, is incorrect. Obviously, having the entire section tap its feet to help the flute player blend in would be ineffective, so answer D is incorrect. At the same time, answer B, ordering the flue player to stop entirely, is unnecessary. Not all musicians have the ability to keep their feet still during their performances and practices, and asking one who needs some motion to keep time would be unnecessary and effective.

67. B: A conductor should practice his or her conducting style in front of a mirror along with taped or recorded music in order to make sure his or her conducting style is rhythmic and appropriate. As awkward as this practice may seem, conductors should practice their batons in much the same way their students practice their instruments: regularly, so their performance adds to the work of the group. Additionally, a conductor *does* add to the quality of the ensemble's musical performance. A good conductor can signal information to musicians regarding a wide variety of musical output including the tempo, rhythm, *and* style, which means that answer D is incorrect. For the same reasons, answer A is incorrect, because conductors' performances are not for show and help the ensemble to perform. Still, the conductor's style is not the audience's primary focus; therefore, answer D is incorrect.

68. D: Practice rooms are rarely used, except for before and after school and, as such, run the risk of being used for storage or becoming eyesores. They have value, however, and should be used, despite their considerable cost to build and maintain. Answer B is incorrect, because practice rooms should use indirect lighting, or lighting projected from the rear, to aid the reading of music without eyestrain. Answer C is incorrect because practice rooms should always include an electronic tuner.

69. C: The piccolo uses less air, but the musician must blow that air more rapidly. The piccolo is smaller than its lower-pitch cousin, the flute; therefore, the piccolo requires less air to work. Nonetheless, since that air is going to be generating notes that are higher in pitch, the air must move with greater speed. Although the piccolo is different from the flute in many ways both subtle and overt, it is similar enough that a flutist with sufficient skill should be able to play it. Therefore, answer A is incorrect. Also incorrect is answer B, because the instrument widely in use today is the C piccolo; the D-flat instrument was used long ago. Finally, the piccolo is known for having *less* pitch flexibility than its larger cousin, so answer D is incorrect.

70. B: Both instruments are pitched to B-flat. While the euphonium and baritone have many features in common, they are different instruments, making the other three possible answers to this question incorrect. First, answer A is incorrect on its face, as both the euphonium and baritone use bass clef, not treble. Secondly, most euphoniums come with four valves, and while four-valve baritone models are made, most baritones in this country come with three valves. Therefore, answer C is incorrect, as is answer D, because the euphonium requires a larger mouthpiece than the baritone.

71. A: The number of tuba players in a band is entirely up to the number of players who want to play it and the desires of the band director. While there are disagreements, as always, regarding the "ideal" number of tubas in an ensemble, the number should depend entirely on the type of sound for which the band director is looking, plus the number of students willing to play this instrument. Anyone who is interested can play the tuba, regardless of size, so answer C is incorrect. Also incorrect is answer B, because while size is unimportant in deciding which students should play the tuba, its sound demands a player who can discern the differences between the lower tones. Finally, modern tubas are made in several keys including F, E-flat, CC, and BB-flat. So, answer D is incorrect.

72. C: A middle school percussion ensemble needs about half the instruments of a high school section. A middle school is probably smaller than the high school into which it feeds, and has fewer band musicians, so a smaller section with fewer instruments is probably fine. Nonetheless, at the same time younger percussionists need experience on the more "tonal" instruments such as marimbas and xylophones, so answer B is incorrect. Also incorrect is answer A, as the needs of the middle school section are smaller in size and scope. Finally, answer D is incorrect, since a middle school section should include instruments such as timpani and bass drums.

73. D: Violins come in full, 1/32, 1/16, 1/8, ¼, ½, and 3/4 sizes, in order to accommodate the wide range of hand and student sizes. As such, all other answers, A, B, and C, are incorrect.

74. B: Extrinsic rewards (such as prizes and certificates) should be awarded only to routine tasks, such as cleaning a rehearsal space or learning more scales than were assigned. Rewards for accomplishing more complex, musically related tasks should be more *intrinsic*, which is to say, from within. Praise, especially in front of a student's peers, would count as intrinsic motivation, as would the sense of satisfaction a student should feel upon solving a complex task. Yet, extrinsic motivation does have a place in most classrooms, so answer A is incorrect. Answer C also is incorrect, as previously stated. Finally, answer D is incorrect, since systems of rewards generally are left to the teacher's discernment and are rarely banned if they do not detract from the learning environment.

75. C: Because a march should *not* feature slowed down tempos when playing softer dynamics. The rest of the answers—up beat accompaniment, 2/4 time, independent bass line—are all characteristics of a march that band directors should know.

Copyright © Mometrix Media. You have been licensed one copy of this document for personal use only. Any other reproduction or redistribution is strictly prohibited. All rights reserved.

76. C: Students should practice a half-hour a so a day, then ideally work up to more than an hour every day. All students, regardless of age and experience, should learn the value and importance of daily practice; a shorter time period, such as a half hour, can start good habits without being overwhelming. By the time the student has gotten older and gained more experience, an hour or more a day of practice would be ideal. Nonetheless, because an hour a day from the beginning will seem overwhelming to a beginner, answer A is incorrect. Also incorrect is answer B, because practice from the beginning of a musical career will help ensure that the career in question will continue to grow, regardless of age or experience. Finally, answer D is incorrect, as inconsistent amounts and qualities of practice will quickly break down. The amount of practice every day should be roughly the same, regardless of the student's mood or repertoire.

77. A: Record the work. Once a piece is recorded, it is considered copyright protected. This is automatic without any of the other steps listed as possible answers. While having a piece of music published, answer B, or registered with the Copyright Office, answer C, gives the composer the advantage of having his or her work registered, these steps are not necessary for the work to be considered protected. Answer D, performing the work, is not a guarantee of copyright, so answer D is incorrect.

78. A: Upper voices and percussion should decrescendo more quickly than lower voices. This allows the lower voices to retain some sense of balance during the decrescendo. Lower voices should crescendo more quickly than upper voices, so answer D is incorrect. Also incorrect is answer B, since percussion should start a crescendo more slowly, then rapidly get louder about a third of the way from the end. Answer C is incorrect, because ensembles should actually drop their volume slightly before the beginning of the crescendo to capture its full power.

79. C: Tenor saxophones should sit near the euphoniums since they often play the same tenor line. The guiding principle in setting up an ensemble's seating is that various instruments should be able to hear what their fellow musicians are playing. As such, first chairs should be seated close to each other or at least on the same side of an orchestra to hear what they are doing with their portion of the piece, in order to better play off of each other. Therefore, answer A is incorrect, as is answer B, because Cornet I and Trumpet I should hear each other above the music of the other horns. Finally, three students per music stand is too many; the number of students per stand should be two or one. As a result, answer D is incorrect.

80. A: No exceptions should be made, even to parents. No student should ever ride home from a school-sponsored event in a car driven by any teen-ager, even if the driver is a relative. While parents theoretically could be considered safe transport even in this litigious era, a consistent policy is best. Parents should know ahead of time that because the student is at a school-sponsored event, the school is responsible for that student's safety from the time the bus leaves the school to the time it returns home. An unbreakable, bus-only policy is not only the easiest to apply in all cases, it is the safest for all persons involved.

81. C: To test concepts such as time and key signatures, music symbols, and musical history. While many music teachers no doubt would prefer to devote their limited time and energy resources to student rehearsal and performance, some assessment of basic student knowledge is necessary. This is especially true if that knowledge can be placed in the context of rehearsal, practice, and performance. The goal of any educational experience should be greater understanding, and written exams provide one more tool a music instructor can use to that end. Since there is a place for written exams in musical education, answer A is incorrect. More advanced students also need to have their more advanced music put into context, so they also can benefit from written work. Therefore, answer B is incorrect, as well, as is answer d. Letter

grades and other rubrics should be based on a number of factors such as performance, improvement, and participation, not just written work.

82. D: Competitions for chair placement should be held both with advance notice and at unannounced times. Periodic competitions for first chair and so on keep more advanced students playing at their best level; many students further down the row will strive to improve their play in order to catch up. The result is a better orchestra. Therefore, answer B is incorrect; while a student's self-esteem is important, all musicians should be able to withstand the pressure of demonstrating their skills to their peers and their instructor. Accordingly, both announced and unannounced competitions have their place in this process. Daily competitions, answer A, would obviously be excessive in a student orchestra's busy schedule. Answer C, conversely, would not put *enough* motivation or pressure on the students to improve.

83. B: Hand vibrato. Beginning trumpet players can be taught easily to add vibrato to the tone their instruments make. All they need to do is move their thumb back and forth as they use their hand to brace their fingers on the valves. Answer A, voice vibrato, is incorrect, as one does not use the vocal cords when playing the trumpet. Answer C, jaw vibrato also is incorrect, because moving the jaw is not used commonly as a technique for achieving vibrato with the trumpet. Moving the lips, or embouchure, is an accepted technique for achieving vibrato, but it takes more practice and skill than using the hand. As a result, answer D is not the best method for a beginning trumpet player to use in order to achieve vibrato in his or her tone.

84. C: Two-thirds woodwinds and one-third brass. It is generally accepted that clarinets form the backbone of any concert band's sound. Therefore, they should provide most of that sound; a two-thirds-to-one-thirds ratio of clarinets and their woodwind cousins should therefore outnumber the brass instruments by this amount. Therefore, answers A, B, and C—which alter the balance to an unacceptable degree—are all incorrect.

85. D: Make changes to the music, moving some instruments to other instruments' parts, as long as the central integrity of the music is preserved. Enough excess instruments can play the parts of their missing fellows while retaining the essential sound of a piece. Parents should not be coerced into pressuring their children to change something so personal as a musical instrument choice, as this act could turn the students off to music for good. As a result, answer A is incorrect. Student orchestras should welcome all participants, especially when so many students lose interest in music and the arts as they get older, so a "cut" list, answer B, should be regarded as an absolute last resort. As for answer C, a band director will encounter much peer pressure among his or her students already, so avoiding any unnecessary or added peer pressure is preferred.

86. C: Independent projects. Students who have a high innate ability for music should be tasked with independent study and other challenges outside of the regular curriculum, including composition and improvisation. Such instruction offers the best way for such students to develop their skills and possibly become lifelong musicians. Ear training is important, but all musicians also should learn at least the basics of reading music, so answer A is incorrect. Also incorrect is answer B, separating gifted musicians from their more average peers. Keeping gifted musicians involved in regular ensembles challenges their classmates to perform better and develops vital leadership and cooperative qualities in the more adept performers. Finally, answer D is incorrect, as all learners situated far from "the norm" are required by law to have adaptations in all classroom environments.

87. D: A music teacher is permitted to make other accommodations beyond those outlined in a student's IEP. Possible accommodations for hearing impaired student musicians might include allowing them to play instruments that permit the feeling of vibrations, or demonstrating music through performance

rather than recorded samples. These excellent strategies for engaging hearing impaired students may not be listed on the students' IEPs. While aides sometimes are provided to students with profound disabilities, such a provision is not a guarantee. Therefore, answer A is incorrect. Also incorrect—and unethical—is answer B, which implies that hearing impaired students can neither perform nor appreciate music. Many fine hearing-impaired musicians, up to and including Ludwig van Beethoven, have proved this theory false. Finally, answer C, limiting hearing impaired students to kinesthetic instruments such as percussion, would be limiting, discriminatory—and incorrect as an answer to this question.

88. D: The Suzuki method deliberately avoids auditions as a means for judging suitability for instruction. The method's founder, Shin'ichi Suzuki, believed that all children had the ability to learn music the way they learn languages. As such, he felt it would be limiting both to students and to prospective teachers to allow only more capable students to learn music. The method introduces students to music and concepts by ear, introducing notation later. As a result, answer A is incorrect. Since the method has spread from violin and piano to instruments such as the guitar, answer B is incorrect also. Answer C is incorrect, since Suzuki was born in Japan and lived there for most of his life.

89. B: The Kodály Method. Zoltán Kodály, who believed that singing was the most effective way to teach music outside the confines offered by an instrument, founded the Kodály Method. While the other three methods listed might place different amounts of value in singing, only in the Kodály Method does it have such a high initial importance. The Dalcroze method emphasizes teaching music primarily through movement, and the Orff Schulwerk is devoted to a child-centered approach, building the teaching of music by connecting it to a child's world and rituals of play. For this reason, answers A, C, and D, are incorrect.

90. A: Shared mouthpieces should be sterilized before being shared. Some mouthpieces can be sterilized, which is important to prevent the spread of disease between students. Because sterilization in some cases is possible, answer B would be incorrect. Answer C is incorrect because these guidelines do state clearly that mouthpieces should be sterilized. Answer D is incorrect because mouthpieces are not self-sterilizing, and sharing mouthpieces can transmit infection.

91. C: Composition. The Orff-Schulwerk process, which grew out of the observations of German composer Carl Orff (1895-1982), attempts to teach music by capitalizing on children's innate abilities to speak, play, dance, and move. Since answer A, imitation, is the cornerstone of the method, it is incorrect. Answer B, a stage in the process, is also incorrect. Answer D, improvisation, is the final stage of the process by which students spontaneously arrange and perform melodies based on what they are hearing. The third stage, literacy, was not listed, and instead was replaced by answer C, composition. Because composition is not featured in the Orff-Schulwerk process *per se*, C is the correct answer.

92. A: As long as songs that avoid outright Biblical passages and themes are avoided or minimized, gospel music emphasizing broader themes can be included as part of a public school's music curriculum. Answer B asserts that the Supreme Court has issued a final ruling on the constitutionality of using music of a religious origin in the public schools. While cases of these kinds are commonplace in the court system, the Court has not issued a final, definitive ruling on this subject. Therefore, answer B is incorrect. Answer C states that teachers who specialize in gospel may teach classes on the subject in the public schools, which is false. Therefore, answer C is incorrect. Finally, answer D incorrectly asserts that gospel music is primarily a European-American genre. Generations of African-American gospel performers and composers would no doubt dispute this claim. Therefore, answer D is incorrect.

93. B: Would be an appropriate intervention for the horn player in question. High school students, even those in "elite" situations, sometimes will err in their responsibilities, especially those high achievers that may spread themselves too thin between academics and other activities such as music. Because they are

young, they will benefit from discrete reminders about the importance of practice and preparation in music. It would be inappropriate to use the solution suggested by answer A; humiliating a student is never acceptable in any setting, especially not in front of his or her peers. Answer C, doing nothing, would not be appropriate, since practice is important and should be addressed. Finally, answer D, is an inappropriate consequence. Discipline should be applied to groups only when most if not all of the students in question have been involved in the infraction.

94. B: Grades K-4. The association states that a student meets the national singing standards if he or she can sing the song in question with proper tone, pitch, and rhythm. Furthermore, it cites "America the Beautiful" specifically as an appropriate song for assessment of general music students in grades K-4. When assessing pre-school students, the teacher asks the student to pick a favorite song. Therefore, answer A is incorrect. In answer C, 5-8, and answer D, 9-12, it is assumed that the teacher has a wide variety of more advanced songs from which to choose appropriate means of assessment. Accordingly, answers C and D are incorrect.

95. B: Music teachers should be able to sing *or* play a musical instrument. This is one of the areas in which teachers of music to younger children can be considered generalists, and therefore do not have to be able to sing **and** play an instrument at a mastered level. In addition, while teachers working with younger children are held to the same standards as teachers working in upper elementary school through high school, they are expected to have *basic* understanding of many of these standards. Neither Texas state standards nor the state law require teachers to have an advanced music degree from an accredited institution, nor do they put an age requirement of 25 years or older on teachers. Finally, they do not require that music teachers have a professional music background. Therefore, answers A, C, and D are incorrect.

96. A: Never. Under no circumstances should a teacher admit wrongdoing in significant cases, such as those involving misconduct or negligence. Doing so could place a teacher's career, certification, and legal status in jeopardy. Because the school's interest may run counter to that of a teacher, regardless of his or her innocence or culpability, a teacher never should admit wrongdoing until he or she has retained legal counsel, which usually will not be provided by the teacher's school district or school board. Therefore, answers B, C, and D are incorrect.

97. A: Diagnostic assessment is performed at the beginning of a semester and includes auditions for select ensembles. While diagnostic assessment can be used to assess a student's skill level and to judge whether he or she is prepared to enter a more advanced band or choir, it also can be used to determine one or more students' skill levels before the teacher begins selecting the semester's music and planning its lessons. Answer B, an assessment performed in the middle of the semester, would be better termed as a *formative* assessment. Answer B is incorrect. Answer C, a *summative* assessment, would be performed at the end of the semester in order to give a summary assessment of skills the student has been expected to know. Since diagnostic assessments are key to students of virtually every age, answer D, reserving them for college age students, is incorrect.

98. D: Suggesting that the student move his or her lower jaw forward, as long as such a shift is comfortable and does not affect the student's embouchure. Severely altering the orientation of a musician's wrists will not solve the problem and will affect adversely the way he or she uses his or her hands, so answer A is incorrect. Also incorrect is answer B, as requiring all students to have proper bite or orthodontia would be unnecessarily impractical and exclusionary. Nonetheless, the incorrectness of answers A and B do not imply that an overbite or improper orientation of the horn should be acceptable in an ensemble, as it can affect tone and projection. Therefore, answer C is incorrect.

99. D: A simple system such as checks (for meeting the standard) and plusses (for exceeding them). A third symbol, such as an O for approaching the standard, also would be appropriate. Answer A, assigning letter grades, would be appropriate only for older students, and then only as an overall grade. Therefore, answer A is incorrect. Also incorrect is answer B, percentages, since they would be overly detailed and unnecessary to assess the basic process of students so young. Conversely, answer C, which asserts that second graders are too young for assessment, is incorrect, as state and national standards exist for students as young as those of pre-school age.

100. D: Japanese. The taiko is an important feature to Japanese music, from classical to folk to other pieces composed in the present day. It is often played alone or in taiko ensembles. While various styles of drum are important in the other musical styles listed, the taiko is key only to Japanese music; indeed, *taiko* means "drum" in Japanese. As a result, all other answers would be incorrect.

Secret Key #1 - Time is Your Greatest Enemy

Pace Yourself

Wear a watch. At the beginning of the test, check the time (or start a chronometer on your watch to count the minutes), and check the time after every few questions to make sure you are "on schedule."

If you are forced to speed up, do it efficiently. Usually one or more answer choices can be eliminated without too much difficulty. Above all, don't panic. Don't speed up and just begin guessing at random choices. By pacing yourself, and continually monitoring your progress against your watch, you will always know exactly how far ahead or behind you are with your available time. If you find that you are one minute behind on the test, don't skip one question without spending any time on it, just to catch back up. Take 15 fewer seconds on the next four questions, and after four questions you'll have caught back up. Once you catch back up, you can continue working each problem at your normal pace.

Furthermore, don't dwell on the problems that you were rushed on. If a problem was taking up too much time and you made a hurried guess, it must be difficult. The difficult questions are the ones you are most likely to miss anyway, so it isn't a big loss. It is better to end with more time than you need than to run out of time.

Lastly, sometimes it is beneficial to slow down if you are constantly getting ahead of time. You are always more likely to catch a careless mistake by working more slowly than quickly, and among very high-scoring test takers (those who are likely to have lots of time left over), careless errors affect the score more than mastery of material.

Secret Key #2 - Guessing is not Guesswork

You probably know that guessing is a good idea. Unlike other standardized tests, there is no penalty for getting a wrong answer. Even if you have no idea about a question, you still have a 20-25% chance of getting it right.

Most test takers do not understand the impact that proper guessing can have on their score. Unless you score extremely high, guessing will significantly contribute to your final score.

Monkeys Take the Test

What most test takers don't realize is that to insure that 20-25% chance, you have to guess randomly. If you put 20 monkeys in a room to take this test, assuming they answered once per question and behaved themselves, on average they would get 20-25% of the questions correct. Put 20 test takers in the room, and the average will be much lower among guessed questions. Why?

1. The test writers intentionally write deceptive answer choices that "look" right. A test taker has no idea about a question, so he picks the "best looking" answer, which is often wrong. The monkey has no idea what looks good and what doesn't, so it will consistently be right about 20-25% of the time.

2. Test takers will eliminate answer choices from the guessing pool based on a hunch or intuition. Simple but correct answers often get excluded, leaving a 0% chance of being correct. The monkey has no clue, and often gets lucky with the best choice.

This is why the process of elimination endorsed by most test courses is flawed and detrimental to your performance. Test takers don't guess; they make an ignorant stab in the dark that is usually worse than random.

$5 Challenge

Let me introduce one of the most valuable ideas of this course—the $5 challenge:
- *You only mark your "best guess" if you are willing to bet $5 on it.*
- *You only eliminate choices from guessing if you are willing to bet $5 on it.*

Why $5? Five dollars is an amount of money that is small yet not insignificant, and can really add up fast (20 questions could cost you $100). Likewise, each answer choice on one question of the test will have a small impact on your overall score, but it can really add up to a lot of points in the end.

The process of elimination IS valuable. The following shows your chance of guessing it right:

If you eliminate wrong answer choices until only this many remain:	Chance of getting it correct:
1	100%
2	50%
3	33%

However, if you accidentally eliminate the right answer or go on a hunch for an incorrect answer, your chances drop dramatically—to 0%. By guessing among all the answer choices, you are GUARANTEED to have a shot at the right answer.

That's why the $5 test is so valuable. If you give up the advantage and safety of a pure guess, it had better be worth the risk.

What we still haven't covered is how to be sure that whatever guess you make is truly random. Here's the easiest way:
- *Always pick the first answer choice among those remaining.*

Such a technique means that you have decided, **before you see a single test question**, exactly how you are going to guess, and since the order of choices tells you nothing about which one is correct, this guessing technique is perfectly random.

This section is not meant to scare you away from making educated guesses or eliminating choices; you just need to define when a choice is worth eliminating. The $5 test, along with a pre-defined random guessing strategy, is the best way to make sure you reap all of the benefits of guessing.

Secret Key #3 - Practice Smarter, Not Harder

Many test takers delay the test preparation process because they dread the awful amounts of practice time they think necessary to succeed on the test. We have refined an effective method that will take you only a fraction of the time.

There are a number of "obstacles" in the path to success. Among these are answering questions, finishing in time, and mastering test-taking strategies. All must be executed on the day of the test at peak performance, or your score will suffer. The test is a mental marathon that has a large impact on your future.

Just like a marathon runner, it is important to work your way up to the full challenge. So first you just worry about questions, and then time, and finally strategy:

Success Strategy

1. Find a good source for practice tests.
2. If you are willing to make a larger time investment, consider using more than one study guide. Often the different approaches of multiple authors will help you "get" difficult concepts.
3. Take a practice test with no time constraints, with all study helps, "open book." Take your time with questions and focus on applying strategies.
4. Take a practice test with time constraints, with all guides, "open book."
5. Take a final practice test without open material and with time limits.

If you have time to take more practice tests, just repeat step 5. By gradually exposing yourself to the full rigors of the test environment, you will condition your mind to the stress of test day and maximize your success.

Secret Key #4 - Prepare, Don't Procrastinate

Let me state an obvious fact: if you take the test three times, you will probably get three different scores. This is due to the way you feel on test day, the level of preparedness you have, and the version of the test you see. Despite the test writers' claims to the contrary, some versions of the test WILL be easier for you than others.

Since your future depends so much on your score, you should maximize your chances of success. In order to maximize the likelihood of success, you've got to prepare in advance. This means taking practice tests and spending time learning the information and test taking strategies you will need to succeed.

Never go take the actual test as a "practice" test, expecting that you can just take it again if you need to. Take all the practice tests you can on your own, but when you go to take the official test, be prepared, be focused, and do your best the first time!

Secret Key #5 - Test Yourself

Everyone knows that time is money. There is no need to spend too much of your time or too little of your time preparing for the test. You should only spend as much of your precious time preparing as is necessary for you to get the score you need.

Once you have taken a practice test under real conditions of time constraints, then you will know if you are ready for the test or not.

If you have scored extremely high the first time that you take the practice test, then there is not much point in spending countless hours studying. You are already there.

Benchmark your abilities by retaking practice tests and seeing how much you have improved. Once you consistently score high enough to guarantee success, then you are ready.

If you have scored well below where you need, then knuckle down and begin studying in earnest. Check your improvement regularly through the use of practice tests under real conditions. Above all, don't worry, panic, or give up. The key is perseverance!

Then, when you go to take the test, remain confident and remember how well you did on the practice tests. If you can score high enough on a practice test, then you can do the same on the real thing.

General Strategies

The most important thing you can do is to ignore your fears and jump into the test immediately. Do not be overwhelmed by any strange-sounding terms. You have to jump into the test like jumping into a pool—all at once is the easiest way.

Make Predictions

As you read and understand the question, try to guess what the answer will be. Remember that several of the answer choices are wrong, and once you begin reading them, your mind will immediately become cluttered with answer choices designed to throw you off. Your mind is typically the most focused immediately after you have read the question and digested its contents. If you can, try to predict what the correct answer will be. You may be surprised at what you can predict.

Quickly scan the choices and see if your prediction is in the listed answer choices. If it is, then you can be quite confident that you have the right answer. It still won't hurt to check the other answer choices, but most of the time, you've got it!

Answer the Question

It may seem obvious to only pick answer choices that answer the question, but the test writers can create some excellent answer choices that are wrong. Don't pick an answer just because it sounds right, or you believe it to be true. It MUST answer the question. Once you've made your selection, always go back and check it against the question and make sure that you didn't misread the question and that the answer choice does answer the question posed.

Benchmark

After you read the first answer choice, decide if you think it sounds correct or not. If it doesn't, move on to the next answer choice. If it does, mentally mark that answer choice. This doesn't mean that you've definitely selected it as your answer choice, it just means that it's the best you've seen thus far. Go ahead and read the next choice. If the next choice is worse than the one you've already selected, keep going to the next answer choice. If the next choice is better than the choice you've already selected, mentally mark the new answer choice as your best guess.

The first answer choice that you select becomes your standard. Every other answer choice must be benchmarked against that standard. That choice is correct until proven otherwise by another answer choice beating it out. Once you've decided that no other answer choice seems as good, do one final check to ensure that your answer choice answers the question posed.

Valid Information

Don't discount any of the information provided in the question. Every piece of information may be necessary to determine the correct answer. None of the information in the question is there to throw you off (while the answer choices will certainly have information to throw you off). If two seemingly unrelated topics are discussed, don't ignore either. You can be confident there is a relationship, or it wouldn't be included in the question, and you are probably going to have to determine what is that relationship to find the answer.

Avoid "Fact Traps"

Don't get distracted by a choice that is factually true. Your search is for the answer that answers the question. Stay focused and don't fall for an answer that is true but irrelevant. Always go back to the question and make sure you're choosing an answer that actually answers the question and is not just a true statement. An answer can be factually correct, but it MUST answer the question asked. Additionally, two answers can both be seemingly correct, so be sure to read all of the answer choices, and make sure that you get the one that BEST answers the question.

Milk the Question

Some of the questions may throw you completely off. They might deal with a subject you have not been exposed to, or one that you haven't reviewed in years. While your lack of knowledge about the subject will be a hindrance, the question itself can give you many clues that will help you find the correct answer. Read the question carefully and look for clues. Watch particularly for adjectives and nouns describing difficult terms or words that you don't recognize. Regardless of whether you completely understand a word or not, replacing it with a synonym, either provided or one you more familiar with, may help you to understand what the questions are asking. Rather than wracking your mind about specific detailed information concerning a difficult term or word, try to use mental substitutes that are easier to understand.

The Trap of Familiarity

Don't just choose a word because you recognize it. On difficult questions, you may not recognize a number of words in the answer choices. The test writers don't put "make-believe" words on the test, so don't think that just because you only recognize all the words in one answer choice that that answer choice must be correct. If you only recognize words in one answer choice, then focus on that one. Is it correct? Try your best to determine if it is correct. If it is, that's great. If not, eliminate it. Each word and answer choice you eliminate increases your chances of getting the question correct, even if you then have to guess among the unfamiliar choices.

Eliminate Answers

Eliminate choices as soon as you realize they are wrong. But be careful! Make sure you consider all of the possible answer choices. Just because one appears right, doesn't mean that the next one won't be even better! The test writers will usually put more than one good answer choice for every question, so read all of them. Don't worry if you are stuck between two that seem right. By getting down to just two remaining possible choices, your odds are now 50/50. Rather than wasting too much time, play the odds. You are guessing, but guessing wisely because you've been able to knock out some of the answer choices that you know are wrong. If you are eliminating choices and realize that the last answer choice you are left with is also obviously wrong, don't panic. Start over and consider each choice again. There may easily be something that you missed the first time and will realize on the second pass.

Tough Questions

If you are stumped on a problem or it appears too hard or too difficult, don't waste time. Move on! Remember though, if you can quickly check for obviously incorrect answer choices, your chances of guessing correctly are greatly improved. Before you completely give up, at least try to knock out a couple of possible answers. Eliminate what you can and then guess at the remaining answer choices before moving on.

Brainstorm

If you get stuck on a difficult question, spend a few seconds quickly brainstorming. Run through the complete list of possible answer choices. Look at each choice and ask yourself, "Could this answer the question satisfactorily?" Go through each answer choice and consider it independently of the others. By systematically going through all possibilities, you may find something that you would otherwise overlook. Remember though that when you get stuck, it's important to try to keep moving.

Read Carefully

Understand the problem. Read the question and answer choices carefully. Don't miss the question because you misread the terms. You have plenty of time to read each question thoroughly and make sure you understand what is being asked. Yet a happy medium must be attained, so don't waste too much time. You must read carefully, but efficiently.

Face Value

When in doubt, use common sense. Always accept the situation in the problem at face value. Don't read too much into it. These problems will not require you to make huge leaps of logic. The test writers aren't trying to throw you off with a cheap trick. If you have to go beyond creativity and make a leap of logic in order to have an answer choice answer the question, then you should look at the other answer choices. Don't overcomplicate the problem by creating theoretical relationships or explanations that will warp time or space. These are normal problems rooted in reality. It's just that the applicable relationship or explanation may not be readily apparent and you have to figure things out. Use your common sense to interpret anything that isn't clear.

Prefixes

If you're having trouble with a word in the question or answer choices, try dissecting it. Take advantage of every clue that the word might include. Prefixes and suffixes can be a huge help. Usually they allow you to determine a basic meaning. Pre- means before, post- means after, pro - is positive, de- is negative. From these prefixes and suffixes, you can get an idea of the general meaning of the word and try to put it into context. Beware though of any traps. Just because con- is the opposite of pro-, doesn't necessarily mean congress is the opposite of progress!

Hedge Phrases

Watch out for critical hedge phrases, led off with words such as "likely," "may," "can," "sometimes," "often," "almost," "mostly," "usually," "generally," "rarely," and "sometimes." Question writers insert these hedge phrases to cover every possibility. Often an answer choice will be wrong simply because it leaves no room for exception. Unless the situation calls for them, avoid answer choices that have definitive words like "exactly," and "always."

Switchback Words

Stay alert for "switchbacks." These are the words and phrases frequently used to alert you to shifts in thought. The most common switchback word is "but." Others include "although," "however," "nevertheless," "on the other hand," "even though," "while," "in spite of," "despite," and "regardless of."

New Information

Correct answer choices will rarely have completely new information included. Answer choices typically are straightforward reflections of the material asked about and will directly relate to the question. If a new piece of information is included in an answer choice that doesn't even seem to relate to the topic being asked about, then that answer choice is likely incorrect. All of the information needed to answer the question is usually provided for you in the question. You should not have to make guesses that are unsupported or choose answer choices that require unknown information that cannot be reasoned from what is given.

Time Management

On technical questions, don't get lost on the technical terms. Don't spend too much time on any one question. If you don't know what a term means, then odds are you aren't going to get much further since you don't have a dictionary. You should be able to immediately recognize whether or not you know a term. If you don't, work with the other clues that you have—the other answer choices and terms provided—but don't waste too much time trying to figure out a difficult term that you don't know.

Contextual Clues

Look for contextual clues. An answer can be right but not the correct answer. The contextual clues will help you find the answer that is most right and is correct. Understand the context in which a phrase or statement is made. This will help you make important distinctions.

Don't Panic

Panicking will not answer any questions for you; therefore, it isn't helpful. When you first see the question, if your mind goes blank, take a deep breath. Force yourself to mechanically go through the steps of solving the problem using the strategies you've learned.

Pace Yourself

Don't get clock fever. It's easy to be overwhelmed when you're looking at a page full of questions, your mind is full of random thoughts and feeling confused, and the clock is ticking down faster than you would like. Calm down and maintain the pace that you have set for yourself. As long as you are on track by monitoring your pace, you are guaranteed to have enough time for yourself. When you get to the last few minutes of the test, it may seem like you won't have enough time left, but if you only have as many questions as you should have left at that point, then you're right on track!

Answer Selection

The best way to pick an answer choice is to eliminate all of those that are wrong, until only one is left and confirm that is the correct answer. Sometimes though, an answer choice may immediately look right. Be careful! Take a second to make sure that the other choices are not equally obvious. Don't make a hasty mistake. There are only two times that you should stop before checking other answers. First is when you are positive that the answer choice you have selected is correct. Second is when time is almost out and you have to make a quick guess!

Check Your Work

Since you will probably not know every term listed and the answer to every question, it is important that you get credit for the ones that you do know. Don't miss any questions through careless mistakes. If at all possible, try to take a second to look back over your answer selection and make sure you've selected the correct answer choice and haven't made a costly careless mistake (such as marking an answer choice that you didn't mean to mark). The time it takes for this quick double check should more than pay for itself in caught mistakes.

Beware of Directly Quoted Answers

Sometimes an answer choice will repeat word for word a portion of the question or reference section. However, beware of such exact duplication. It may be a trap! More than likely, the correct choice will paraphrase or summarize a point, rather than being exactly the same wording.

Slang

Scientific sounding answers are better than slang ones. An answer choice that begins "To compare the outcomes..." is much more likely to be correct than one that begins "Because some people insisted..."

Extreme Statements

Avoid wild answers that throw out highly controversial ideas that are proclaimed as established fact. An answer choice that states the "process should used in certain situations, if..." is much more likely to be correct than one that states the "process should be discontinued completely." The first is a calm rational statement and doesn't even make a definitive, uncompromising stance, using a hedge word "if" to provide wiggle room, whereas the second choice is a radical idea and far more extreme.

Answer Choice Families

When you have two or more answer choices that are direct opposites or parallels, one of them is usually the correct answer. For instance, if one answer choice states "x increases" and another answer choice states "x decreases" or "y increases," then those two or three answer choices are very similar in construction and fall into the same family of answer choices. A family of answer choices consists of two or three answer choices, very similar in construction, but often with directly opposite meanings. Usually the correct answer choice will be in that family of answer choices. The "odd man out" or answer choice that doesn't seem to fit the parallel construction of the other answer choices is more likely to be incorrect.

Special Report: How to Overcome Test Anxiety

The very nature of tests caters to some level of anxiety, nervousness, or tension, just as we feel for any important event that occurs in our lives. A little bit of anxiety or nervousness can be a good thing. It helps us with motivation, and makes achievement just that much sweeter. However, too much anxiety can be a problem, especially if it hinders our ability to function and perform.

"Test anxiety," is the term that refers to the emotional reactions that some test-takers experience when faced with a test or exam. Having a fear of testing and exams is based upon a rational fear, since the test-taker's performance can shape the course of an academic career. Nevertheless, experiencing excessive fear of examinations will only interfere with the test-taker's ability to perform and chance to be successful.

There are a large variety of causes that can contribute to the development and sensation of test anxiety. These include, but are not limited to, lack of preparation and worrying about issues surrounding the test.

Lack of Preparation

Lack of preparation can be identified by the following behaviors or situations:
- Not scheduling enough time to study, and therefore cramming the night before the test or exam
- Managing time poorly, to create the sensation that there is not enough time to do everything
- Failing to organize the text information in advance, so that the study material consists of the entire text and not simply the pertinent information
- Poor overall studying habits

Worrying, on the other hand, can be related to both the test taker, or many other factors around him/her that will be affected by the results of the test. These include worrying about:
- Previous performances on similar exams, or exams in general
- How friends and other students are achieving
- The negative consequences that will result from a poor grade or failure

There are three primary elements to test anxiety. Physical components, which involve the same typical bodily reactions as those to acute anxiety (to be discussed below). Emotional factors have to do with fear or panic. Mental or cognitive issues concerning attention spans and memory abilities.

Physical Signals

There are many different symptoms of test anxiety, and these are not limited to mental and emotional strain. Frequently there are a range of physical signals that will let a test taker know that he/she is suffering from test anxiety. These bodily changes can include the following:
- Perspiring
- Sweaty palms
- Wet, trembling hands

- Nausea
- Dry mouth
- A knot in the stomach
- Headache
- Faintness
- Muscle tension
- Aching shoulders, back and neck
- Rapid heart beat
- Feeling too hot/cold

To recognize the sensation of test anxiety, a test-taker should monitor him/herself for the following sensations:

- The physical distress symptoms as listed above
- Emotional sensitivity, expressing emotional feelings such as the need to cry or laugh too much, or a sensation of anger or helplessness
- A decreased ability to think, causing the test-taker to blank out or have racing thoughts that are hard to organize or control.

Though most students will feel some level of anxiety when faced with a test or exam, the majority can cope with that anxiety and maintain it at a manageable level. However, those who cannot are faced with a very real and very serious condition, which can and should be controlled for the immeasurable benefit of this sufferer.

Naturally, these sensations lead to negative results for the testing experience. The most common effects of test anxiety have to do with nervousness and mental blocking.

Nervousness

Nervousness can appear in several different levels:

- The test-taker's difficulty, or even inability to read and understand the questions on the test
- The difficulty or inability to organize thoughts to a coherent form
- The difficulty or inability to recall key words and concepts relating to the testing questions (especially essays)
- The receipt of poor grades on a test, though the test material was well known by the test taker

Conversely, a person may also experience mental blocking, which involves:

- Blanking out on test questions
- Only remembering the correct answers to the questions when the test has already finished.

Fortunately for test anxiety sufferers, beating these feelings, to a large degree, has to do with proper preparation. When a test taker has a feeling of preparedness, then anxiety will be dramatically lessened.

The first step to resolving anxiety issues is to distinguish which of the two types of anxiety are being suffered. If the anxiety is a direct result of a lack of preparation, this should be considered a normal reaction, and the anxiety level (as opposed to the test results) shouldn't be anything to worry about. However, if, when adequately prepared, the test-taker still panics, blanks out, or seems to overreact, this is not a fully rational reaction. While this can be considered normal too, there are many ways to combat and overcome these effects.

Remember that anxiety cannot be entirely eliminated, however, there are ways to minimize it, to make the anxiety easier to manage. Preparation is one of the best ways to minimize test anxiety. Therefore the following techniques are wise in order to best fight off any anxiety that may want to build.

To begin with, try to avoid cramming before a test, whenever it is possible. By trying to memorize an entire term's worth of information in one day, you'll be shocking your system, and not giving yourself a very good chance to absorb the information. This is an easy path to anxiety, so for those who suffer from test anxiety, cramming should not even be considered an option.

Instead of cramming, work throughout the semester to combine all of the material which is presented throughout the semester, and work on it gradually as the course goes by, making sure to master the main concepts first, leaving minor details for a week or so before the test.

To study for the upcoming exam, be sure to pose questions that may be on the examination, to gauge the ability to answer them by integrating the ideas from your texts, notes and lectures, as well as any supplementary readings.

If it is truly impossible to cover all of the information that was covered in that particular term, concentrate on the most important portions, that can be covered very well. Learn these concepts as best as possible, so that when the test comes, a goal can be made to use these concepts as presentations of your knowledge.

In addition to study habits, changes in attitude are critical to beating a struggle with test anxiety. In fact, an improvement of the perspective over the entire test-taking experience can actually help a test taker to enjoy studying and therefore improve the overall experience. Be certain not to overemphasize the significance of the grade - know that the result of the test is neither a reflection of self worth, nor is it a measure of intelligence; one grade will not predict a person's future success.

To improve an overall testing outlook, the following steps should be tried:
- Keeping in mind that the most reasonable expectation for taking a test is to expect to try to demonstrate as much of what you know as you possibly can.
- Reminding ourselves that a test is only one test; this is not the only one, and there will be others.
- The thought of thinking of oneself in an irrational, all-or-nothing term should be avoided at all costs.
- A reward should be designated for after the test, so there's something to look forward to. Whether it be going to a movie, going out to eat, or simply visiting friends, schedule it in advance, and do it no matter what result is expected on the exam.

Test-takers should also keep in mind that the basics are some of the most important things, even beyond anti-anxiety techniques and studying. Never neglect the basic social, emotional and biological needs, in order to try to absorb information. In order to best achieve, these three factors must be held as just as important as the studying itself.

Study Steps

Remember the following important steps for studying:
- Maintain healthy nutrition and exercise habits. Continue both your recreational activities and social pass times. These both contribute to your physical and emotional well being.
- Be certain to get a good amount of sleep, especially the night before the test, because when you're overtired you are not able to perform to the best of your best ability.
- Keep the studying pace to a moderate level by taking breaks when they are needed, and varying the work whenever possible, to keep the mind fresh instead of getting bored.
- When enough studying has been done that all the material that can be learned has been learned, and the test taker is prepared for the test, stop studying and do something relaxing such as listening to music, watching a movie, or taking a warm bubble bath.

There are also many other techniques to minimize the uneasiness or apprehension that is experienced along with test anxiety before, during, or even after the examination. In fact, there are a great deal of things that can be done to stop anxiety from interfering with lifestyle and performance. Again, remember that anxiety will not be eliminated entirely, and it shouldn't be. Otherwise that "up" feeling for exams would not exist, and most of us depend on that sensation to perform better than usual. However, this anxiety has to be at a level that is manageable.

Of course, as we have just discussed, being prepared for the exam is half the battle right away. Attending all classes, finding out what knowledge will be expected on the exam, and knowing the exam schedules are easy steps to lowering anxiety. Keeping up with work will remove the need to cram, and efficient study habits will eliminate wasted time. Studying should be done in an ideal location for concentration, so that it is simple to become interested in the material and give it complete attention. A method such as SQ3R (Survey, Question, Read, Recite, Review) is a wonderful key to follow to make sure that the study habits are as effective as possible, especially in the case of learning from a textbook. Flashcards are great techniques for memorization. Learning to take good notes will mean that notes will be full of useful information, so that less sifting will need to be done to seek out what is pertinent for studying. Reviewing notes after class and then again on occasion will keep the information fresh in the mind. From notes that have been taken summary sheets and outlines can be made for simpler reviewing.

A study group can also be a very motivational and helpful place to study, as there will be a sharing of ideas, all of the minds can work together, to make sure that everyone understands, and the studying will be made more interesting because it will be a social occasion.

Basically, though, as long as the test-taker remains organized and self confident, with efficient study habits, less time will need to be spent studying, and higher grades will be achieved.

To become self confident, there are many useful steps. The first of these is "self talk." It has been shown through extensive research, that self-talk for students who suffer from test anxiety, should be well monitored, in order to make sure that it contributes to self confidence as opposed to sinking the student. Frequently the self talk of test-anxious students is negative or self-defeating, thinking that everyone else is smarter and faster, that they always mess up, and that if they don't do well, they'll fail the entire course. It is important to decreasing anxiety that awareness is made of self talk. Try writing any negative self thoughts and then disputing them with a positive statement instead. Begin self-encouragement as though it was a friend speaking. Repeat positive statements to help reprogram the mind to believing in successes instead of failures.

Helpful Techniques

Other extremely helpful techniques include:

- Self-visualization of doing well and reaching goals
- While aiming for an "A" level of understanding, don't try to "overprotect" by setting your expectations lower. This will only convince the mind to stop studying in order to meet the lower expectations.
- Don't make comparisons with the results or habits of other students. These are individual factors, and different things work for different people, causing different results.
- Strive to become an expert in learning what works well, and what can be done in order to improve. Consider collecting this data in a journal.
- Create rewards for after studying instead of doing things before studying that will only turn into avoidance behaviors.
- Make a practice of relaxing - by using methods such as progressive relaxation, self-hypnosis, guided imagery, etc - in order to make relaxation an automatic sensation.
- Work on creating a state of relaxed concentration so that concentrating will take on the focus of the mind, so that none will be wasted on worrying.
- Take good care of the physical self by eating well and getting enough sleep.
- Plan in time for exercise and stick to this plan.

Beyond these techniques, there are other methods to be used before, during and after the test that will help the test-taker perform well in addition to overcoming anxiety.

Before the exam comes the academic preparation. This involves establishing a study schedule and beginning at least one week before the actual date of the test. By doing this, the anxiety of not having enough time to study for the test will be automatically eliminated. Moreover, this will make the studying a much more effective experience, ensuring that the learning will be an easier process. This relieves much undue pressure on the test-taker.

Summary sheets, note cards, and flash cards with the main concepts and examples of these main concepts should be prepared in advance of the actual studying time. A topic should never be eliminated from this process. By omitting a topic because it isn't expected to be on the test is only setting up the test-taker for anxiety should it actually appear on the exam. Utilize the course syllabus for laying out the topics that should be studied. Carefully go over the notes that were made in class, paying special attention to any of the issues that the professor took special care to emphasize while lecturing in class. In the textbooks, use the chapter review, or if possible, the chapter tests, to begin your review.

It may even be possible to ask the instructor what information will be covered on the exam, or what the format of the exam will be (for example, multiple choice, essay, free form, true-false). Additionally, see if it is possible to find out how many questions will be on the test. If a review sheet or sample test has been offered by the professor, make good use of it, above anything else, for the preparation for the test. Another great resource for getting to know the examination is reviewing tests from previous semesters. Use these tests to review, and aim to achieve a 100% score on each of the possible topics. With a few exceptions, the goal that you set for yourself is the highest one that you will reach.

Take all of the questions that were assigned as homework, and rework them to any other possible course material. The more problems reworked, the more skill and confidence will form as a result.

When forming the solution to a problem, write out each of the steps. Don't simply do head work. By doing as many steps on paper as possible, much clarification and therefore confidence will be formed. Do this with as many homework problems as possible, before checking the answers. By checking the answer after each problem, a reinforcement will exist, that will not be on the exam. Study situations should be as exam-like as possible, to prime the test-taker's system for the experience. By waiting to check the answers at the end, a psychological advantage will be formed, to decrease the stress factor.

Another fantastic reason for not cramming is the avoidance of confusion in concepts, especially when it comes to mathematics. 8-10 hours of study will become one hundred percent more effective if it is spread out over a week or at least several days, instead of doing it all in one sitting. Recognize that the human brain requires time in order to assimilate new material, so frequent breaks and a span of study time over several days will be much more beneficial.

Additionally, don't study right up until the point of the exam. Studying should stop a minimum of one hour before the exam begins. This allows the brain to rest and put things in their proper order. This will also provide the time to become as relaxed as possible when going into the examination room. The test-taker will also have time to eat well and eat sensibly. Know that the brain needs food as much as the rest of the body. With enough food and enough sleep, as well as a relaxed attitude, the body and the mind are primed for success.

Avoid any anxious classmates who are talking about the exam. These students only spread anxiety, and are not worth sharing the anxious sentimentalities.

Before the test also involves creating a positive attitude, so mental preparation should also be a point of concentration. There are many keys to creating a positive attitude. Should fears become rushing in, make a visualization of taking the exam, doing well, and seeing an A written on the paper. Write out a list of affirmations that will bring a feeling of confidence, such as "I am doing well in my English class," "I studied well and know my material," "I enjoy this class." Even if the affirmations aren't believed at first, it sends a positive message to the subconscious which will result in an alteration of the overall belief system, which is the system that creates reality.

If a sensation of panic begins, work with the fear and imagine the very worst! Work through the entire scenario of not passing the test, failing the entire course, and dropping out of school, followed by not getting a job, and pushing a shopping cart through the dark alley where you'll live. This will place things into perspective! Then, practice deep breathing and create a visualization of the opposite situation - achieving an "A" on the exam, passing the entire course, receiving the degree at a graduation ceremony.

On the day of the test, there are many things to be done to ensure the best results, as well as the most calm outlook. The following stages are suggested in order to maximize test-taking potential:
- Begin the examination day with a moderate breakfast, and avoid any coffee or beverages with caffeine if the test taker is prone to jitters. Even people who are used to managing caffeine can feel jittery or light-headed when it is taken on a test day.
- Attempt to do something that is relaxing before the examination begins. As last minute cramming clouds the mastering of overall concepts, it is better to use this time to create a calming outlook.
- Be certain to arrive at the test location well in advance, in order to provide time to select a location that is away from doors, windows and other distractions, as well as giving enough time to relax before the test begins.

- Keep away from anxiety generating classmates who will upset the sensation of stability and relaxation that is being attempted before the exam.
- Should the waiting period before the exam begins cause anxiety, create a self-distraction by reading a light magazine or something else that is relaxing and simple.

During the exam itself, read the entire exam from beginning to end, and find out how much time should be allotted to each individual problem. Once writing the exam, should more time be taken for a problem, it should be abandoned, in order to begin another problem. If there is time at the end, the unfinished problem can always be returned to and completed.

Read the instructions very carefully - twice - so that unpleasant surprises won't follow during or after the exam has ended.

When writing the exam, pretend that the situation is actually simply the completion of homework within a library, or at home. This will assist in forming a relaxed atmosphere, and will allow the brain extra focus for the complex thinking function.

Begin the exam with all of the questions with which the most confidence is felt. This will build the confidence level regarding the entire exam and will begin a quality momentum. This will also create encouragement for trying the problems where uncertainty resides.

Going with the "gut instinct" is always the way to go when solving a problem. Second guessing should be avoided at all costs. Have confidence in the ability to do well.

For essay questions, create an outline in advance that will keep the mind organized and make certain that all of the points are remembered. For multiple choice, read every answer, even if the correct one has been spotted - a better one may exist.

Continue at a pace that is reasonable and not rushed, in order to be able to work carefully. Provide enough time to go over the answers at the end, to check for small errors that can be corrected.

Should a feeling of panic begin, breathe deeply, and think of the feeling of the body releasing sand through its pores. Visualize a calm, peaceful place, and include all of the sights, sounds and sensations of this image. Continue the deep breathing, and take a few minutes to continue this with closed eyes. When all is well again, return to the test.

If a "blanking" occurs for a certain question, skip it and move on to the next question. There will be time to return to the other question later. Get everything done that can be done, first, to guarantee all the grades that can be compiled, and to build all of the confidence possible. Then return to the weaker questions to build the marks from there.

Remember, one's own reality can be created, so as long as the belief is there, success will follow. And remember: anxiety can happen later, right now, there's an exam to be written!

After the examination is complete, whether there is a feeling for a good grade or a bad grade, don't dwell on the exam, and be certain to follow through on the reward that was promised...and enjoy it! Don't dwell on any mistakes that have been made, as there is nothing that can be done at this point anyway.

Additionally, don't begin to study for the next test right away. Do something relaxing for a while, and let the mind relax and prepare itself to begin absorbing information again.

From the results of the exam - both the grade and the entire experience, be certain to learn from what has gone on. Perfect studying habits and work some more on confidence in order to make the next examination experience even better than the last one.

Learn to avoid places where openings occurred for laziness, procrastination and day dreaming.

Use the time between this exam and the next one to better learn to relax, even learning to relax on cue, so that any anxiety can be controlled during the next exam. Learn how to relax the body. Slouch in your chair if that helps. Tighten and then relax all of the different muscle groups, one group at a time, beginning with the feet and then working all the way up to the neck and face. This will ultimately relax the muscles more than they were to begin with. Learn how to breathe deeply and comfortably, and focus on this breathing going in and out as a relaxing thought. With every exhale, repeat the word "relax."

As common as test anxiety is, it is very possible to overcome it. Make yourself one of the test-takers who overcome this frustrating hindrance.

Additional Bonus Material

Due to our efforts to try to keep this book to a manageable length, we've created a link that will give you access to all of your additional bonus material.

Please visit http://www.mometrix.com/bonus948/ftcemusic to access the information.